THE NATIONAL INSTITUTE OF
ECONOMIC AND SOCIAL RESEARCH

Occasional Papers
XXXII

CONCENTRATION IN
BRITISH INDUSTRY
1935-75

CONCENTRATION
IN BRITISH INDUSTRY
1935–75

A study of the growth, causes and effects of
concentration in British manufacturing industries

P. E. HART and R. CLARKE

CAMBRIDGE UNIVERSITY PRESS

CAMBRIDGE

LONDON   NEW YORK   NEW ROCHELLE

MELBOURNE   SYDNEY

Published by the Press Syndicate of the University of Cambridge
The Pitt Building, Trumpington Street, Cambridge CB2 1RP
32 East 57th Street, New York, NY 10022, USA
296 Beaconsfield Parade, Middle Park, Melbourne 3206, Australia

First published 1980

Filmset by Keyspools Ltd,
Golborne, Lancs

Printed and bound in Great Britain
at The Pitman Press, Bath

British Library Cataloguing in Publication Data
Hart, Peter Edward
Concentration in British industry, 1935–75. – (National Institute
of Economic and Social Research. Occasional papers; 32).
1. Industrial concentration – Great Britain – History –
20th century
I. Title II. Clarke, Roger III. Series
338.8   HD731.5   79–41808
ISBN 0 521 23393 3

CONTENTS

Contents

Contents

Note

The following appendices are available in the Institute's
Discussion Paper series:

TABLES

SYMBOLS IN THE TABLES

...	not available
—	nil or negligible
n.a.	not applicable

CHART

PREFACE

This book forms part of a series of studies of business concentration undertaken at the National Institute of Economic and Social Research. Since its foundation, the National Institute has maintained a keen interest in the economic problems of industrial structure, but its research on business concentration dates from the mid-1950s. This was the time when a small proportion of the counterpart funds of Marshall Aid was devoted to economic research on the lack of competition, and on the associated low productivity, which was then thought to typify British industry. The National Institute was fortunate enough to obtain financial assistance from this American source to support a two-year research project on business concentration in the United Kingdom.

At that time, the reliable information for the United Kingdom related to 1935 and was contained in the seminal paper by Leak and Maizels.[1] This was the starting point for the National Institute project. Additional guidelines were provided by the classic studies of business concentration in America which naturally had a profound influence on the small team of research workers at the National Institute.[2] As a result, this team divided its research effort into two main lines of investigation. The first followed the route indicated by Berle and Means and was directed at the measurement of long-term changes in the share of the two hundred top enterprises in British manufacturing. This may be termed 'the aggregate approach'. The second followed that of the National Resources Committee and the Temporary National Economic Committee and was concerned with measuring the shares of the three largest enterprises in each industry. This may be termed the 'disaggregated approach'.

The first or aggregate approach soon passed from the share of the top two hundred to an investigation of the whole size distribution, or at least that part of it which could be measured, and the results were published in

---

[1] H. Leak and A. Maizels, 'The structure of British industry', *Journal of the Royal Statistical Society* (series A), vol. 108, parts 1 and 2, 1945.

[2] A. A. Berle and G. C. Means, *The Modern Corporation and Private Property*, New York, Macmillan, 1932; National Resources Committee, *The Structure of the American Economy*, US Government Printing Office, 1939, prepared under the direction of G. C. Means; Reports of the Temporary National Economic Committee on the *Concentration of Economic Power*, US Government Printing Office, 1940–2.

a paper by Hart and Prais.[1] This paper was criticised at the time by Blair,[2] a former student of Means, for its use of stochastic models.

I would like at least to express the hope that economic concentration and the measurement thereof will not, as has been happening to so many economic topics, become the plaything of the mathematicians who have been invading the dismal science. Because of its importance in economic thought and public policy, it would be tragic if future analyses of concentration were to be nothing more than exercises in the manipulation of symbols. The subject is too important to deserve the fate of a return to medieval scholasticism.

In our view this criticism was unjustified then. It is certainly unjustified now, for in a recent National Institute volume Prais has explained at length the precise economic significance of the statistical models of the proportionate growth of firms of different sizes.[3]

The second or disaggregated approach led to the National Institute book by Evely and Little.[4] Parts I and II of this authoritative work contained a statistical analysis of concentration at the level of individual industries, 1935–51, and part III contained a series of case studies of individual trades. In the early 1970s the National Institute decided to update the work by Evely and Little. It published the results of the new descriptive case studies, corresponding to part III of Evely and Little, in two Occasional Papers.[5] The updating and extension of parts I and II of Evely and Little takes place in the present volume, which is primarily concerned with the statistical analysis of concentration at the level of individual industries. That is, it analyses the level and changes in industry concentration ratios, defined as the share of the five top enterprises in an industry's employment (or output or sales), on the grounds that such ratios give a good indication of the degree of monopoly in an industry.

The relationship between concentration ratios and market power, which has been the subject of debate, was reviewed by Hart, Utton and Walshe and there is no point in repeating all the arguments here: suffice it to say that the concentration ratio is the least unsatisfactory measure of the degree of monopoly available, but because of its many shortcomings it must be supplemented by case studies which can include all the restraints on competition outside the measuring rod of the concentration ratio.

[1] P. E. Hart and S. J. Prais, 'The analysis of business concentration: a statistical approach', *Journal of the Royal Statistical Society* (series A), vol. 119, part 2, 1956.
[2] J. M. Blair, 'Statistical measures of concentration in business', *Bulletin of the Oxford University Institute of Statistics*, vol. 18, 1956.
[3] S. J. Prais, *The Evolution of Giant Firms in Britain*, Cambridge University Press, 1976.
[4] R. Evely and I. M. D. Little, *Concentration in British Industry*, Cambridge University Press, 1960.
[5] P. E. Hart, M. A. Utton and G. Walshe, *Mergers and Concentration in British Industry*, Cambridge University Press, 1973; G. Walshe, *Recent Trends in Monopoly in Great Britain*, Cambridge University Press, 1974.

However, for the purpose of measuring broad tendencies in many industries, the concentration ratio is adequate enough. It is true that there are many alternative measures of concentration; indeed in recent years there has arisen a flourishing cottage industry producing such measures. But there is no need to analyse them in the present volume, for a critical review of them has been published separately.[1]

In addition to measuring average levels and changes in industrial concentration, the present volume examines the causes and economic consequences of these trends. In one sense these industry concentration ratios disaggregate the share of the hundred largest enterprises in total manufacturing investigated by Prais. But this disaggregation brings with it a host of different economic problems associated with pricing, profit-margins, labour payments, and efficiency, in addition to those created by mergers, by economies of scale and by 'spontaneous drift' or stochastic processes. The latter are as important for an individual industry as for the aggregate of all manufacturing industries. But the primary object of this book is to measure and discuss the systematic forces affecting industrial concentration, and the fact that little use is made of the stochastic models of Gibrat or of Galton simply means that we have nothing to add to the discussion of such processes to be found in Prais.

Prais also analyses the financial forces which favour the growth of giant firms. These forces obviously contribute to industrial concentration but they operate on all firms across all industries, whereas the present volume is concerned primarily with concentration *within* individual industries: a large firm can grow very rapidly by taking over firms in other industries without necessarily increasing the degree of monopoly in any one of the industries involved and, while this growth would pose interesting problems, they would differ in character from the traditional economic problems of monopoly pricing, profitability, efficiency and the like. Such problems are the subject of this volume.

One link between the two approaches to the study of business concentration occurs in research on the increasing diversification of large firms across several industries. This diversification takes place not only through the mechanism of takeovers, but also through the internal growth of a large firm which, for example, may decide to form a subsidiary company to make a new product, or to make an old product formerly

---

[1] P. E. Hart, 'Moment distributions in economics: an exposition', *Journal of the Royal Statistical Society* (series A), vol. 138, part 3, 1975. Recent reviews have been provided by J. C. Hause, 'The measurement of concentrated industrial structure and the size distribution of firms', *Annals of Economic and Social Measurement*, vol. 6, 1977, and R. Schmalensee, 'Using the *H*-index of concentration with published data', *Review of Economics and Statistics*, vol. 59, 1977. They show that the correlation between the concentration ratio and other measures of concentration is not always very high. They prefer the Hirschman–Herfindahl, *H*-index. We prefer the concentration ratio, for the reasons given in appendix 1A.

supplied to it by another company. There are many methods of diversification and, although each one of them has some relevance for the degree of concentration at the industry level, they are not studied here; however, they form the subject matter of a third National Institute study.[1]

These three research projects were undertaken to provide a general understanding of the forces affecting industrial structure and to assist in the formation of government policy towards the private sector of industry. The Monopolies Commission, the Office of Fair Trading, the Price Commission are three examples of government intervention in industry and it is obviously better for them to base their policies on empirical research than on the intuition of the politicians of the day or on the untested theories of 'some academic scribbler of a few years back'.[2] Thus while our book does not comment on government policy towards industry, it is intended to provide a useful background for those directly concerned with the formation of this policy, whether they be businessmen or civil servants.

The fact that Sigbert Prais and Michael Utton have been working on research projects so closely related to ours has meant that we have gained a tremendous amount from discussions with them. Their extensive comments on our earlier draft have been invaluable and it is a pleasure to record our thanks to them. We are also very grateful for the most helpful comments on earlier drafts from David Worswick, the Director of the National Institute, Stephen Davies of the University of Sheffield, formerly on the staff at the Institute, Ken George of University College Cardiff and Paul Geroski of Southampton University. We also wish to thank Kit Jones, Secretary of the Institute, for organising the publication of the book, Alison Rowlatt for preparing the text for the printer and compiling the index, Muriel Hill and Pam Watts who carried out the numerical calculations and Angela Manfield who typed the successive drafts.

The study has been financed mainly by a grant from the Office of Fair Trading which we gratefully acknowledge.

National Institute of Economic and Social Research
October 1979

P. E. HART
R. CLARKE

[1] M. A. Utton, *Diversification and Competition*, Cambridge University Press, 1979.
[2] J. M. Keynes, *The General Theory of Employment, Interest and Money*, London, Macmillan, 1936, p. 383.

INTRODUCTION

THE ECONOMIC PROBLEMS OF INDUSTRIAL CONCENTRATION

Manufacturing business in the United Kingdom has become concentrated under the control of fewer and fewer firms. This trend has been observed for manufacturing as a whole: the share of the hundred largest enterprises in total manufacturing net output increased from about 16 per cent in 1909 to about 41 per cent by 1970.[1] It also applied to the average of the individual manufacturing industries for which more detailed observations are available since 1935. For example, the share of the three largest enterprises in the total employment of the average industry in 1973 was 42 per cent compared with 29 per cent in 1951. The increase in concentration at the industry level has been regarded as indicating a steady drift away from atomistic competition and as casting doubt on economic policies which rest on the assumption that competition is the rule in the private sector of manufacturing industry. The extent of this drift together with its causes and its effects form the subject matter of this book.

The principal tool of analysis employed in this book is the 'concentration ratio', which gives the share of the largest enterprises in the employment or sales of a particular industry or product. Thus, if in a particular industry the three largest enterprises employed 50,000 people out of a total industry employment of 125,000, the three-enterprise employment concentration for that industry, denoted by C_3, would be 40 per cent. The average of such concentration ratios for all manufacturing industries would then be an inverse measure of the state of competition in manufacturing industry. Calculations of such averages at different points in time may then be used to gauge the trend in industrial competition over time which is widely believed to be a major determinant of an industry's economic performance, especially in terms of its average efficiency. If these beliefs were justified, the implications for economic policy would be clear enough: encourage more competition and the decline in the efficiency of British manufacturing industry compared with that of its overseas competitors would be halted and even reversed.

---

[1] Prais, *Evolution of Giant Firms*.

Let us turn now to the definition of an industry. In economic theory, an industry is a collection of firms making products which are highly substitutable; formally, they have high cross-elasticities of demand or supply. In practice we have to use the definitions of the basic source of data, the Census of Production, which may not always correspond very closely to the economists' theoretical concept. In this study we use two census definitions. First, the industry or minimum list heading (MLH), which is similar to the three-digit level of aggregation in international statistical parlance. Most census data are classified by MLH and most of our statistical analysis must be based on this classification. However, census industries comprise groups of products with common supply characteristics, but which are sometimes too heterogeneous from the point of view of demand to match the definition of an industry in economic theory. A closer approximation is sometimes obtained by using a second census definition based on a relatively homogeneous principal product, which roughly corresponds to the four-digit level of aggregation in international statistics. The census product data are less comprehensive than the industry data, and since neither set is superior in all cases, we use both in this book and compare the results.

THE METHODOLOGICAL APPROACH

The fundamental approach of this study is empirical. In the words of Stigler:[1]

The quantitative, or better, empirical study of economic life is the only way in which one can get a real feeling for the tasks and functioning of an economic system. The completely formal theorist does not know the range or subtlety of the economic problems that arise each day, for a man is not as resourceful or imaginative as a society of men. The formal theorist therefore has a much simplified picture of the world and of the complexity of the scientific theorems required to explain its operation. He fails to realize the extent to which the successful explanation of the workings of the economy demands an enlarged scientific technique, judgment, and information, whereas the experienced empirical worker has had the complexities of the economy burned into his soul.

The extensive use of statistics in the present work, and of descriptive case studies in the companion volumes already published, does not mean that we are adopting a 'bucket theory of knowledge', to use the terminology of Popper.[2] By describing our methodological approach as empirical we simply mean that the chapters are usually descriptive and statistical, while the relevant economic theory is not given much emphasis.

---

[1] G. J. Stigler, *Essays in the History of Economics*, University of Chicago Press, 1965.
[2] K. R. Popper, *Objective Knowledge*, Oxford, Clarendon Press, 1972, p. 61.

Moreover, when the relevant economic theory is discussed, it is not always the standard neoclassical microeconomic theory used by so many writers on monopoly problems. Sometimes we revert to an older classical notion of competition with its greater emphasis on the dynamic process of rivalry between firms. Whilst neoclassical microeconomic theory places emphasis on the number and size distribution of firms as the crucial determinants of economic performance in a static sense, this method of approach may in some instances be too narrow. For example, neoclassical theory implies that industries with high concentration ratios have high mark-ups of price over marginal cost. This essentially static prediction assumes away some of the most important problems. For example it is widely believed that oligopolists pursue other goals such as sales or utility maximisation or that they adopt rules of thumb in setting prices rather than strictly maximise profits. They may tolerate more inefficiency, be slower in transferring resources from one use to another following changes in demand, be more ready to accept restrictive labour practices and even pass on part of their monopoly rents to labour in the form of higher wages. Competition in the sense of rivalry over such matters as prices, product quality or after-sales service may actually be keener among a few large firms than among numerous smaller firms. Similarly, incentives to research and development and innovation may be stronger when large firms are able to appropriate more of the gains from such activities. The actual market structure in an industry at a particular time may then be an inadequate guide to profit-margins in that industry in that it fails to take account of the very complex nature of actual competition.

This does not mean that we ignore neoclassical theory: it simply means that it is sometimes subordinated to more relevant theory. The great virtue of neoclassical microeconomic theory is that it provides a preliminary framework for analysing economic problems and this framework, which is familiar to all economists, provides a common starting-point and sometimes provides useful insights and checks on consistency. For example, neoclassical theory implies that the price elasticity of demand affects the margin between prices and costs. Thus empirical studies purporting to explain variation in price–cost margins between industries should include this elasticity, or its equivalent, among the explanatory variables. Some empirical studies relying entirely on *ad hoc* theoretical specifications have not only omitted it but seem to be unaware that it ought to be included.

Nevertheless neoclassical theory is insufficient because it is both static and deterministic, whereas in the real world dynamic and stochastic forces have powerful effects on the degree of industrial concentration. The dynamic nature of competition has been noted already. The stochastic character of industrial structure needs a word of explanation. Briefly, the change in the degree of concentration, measured by the proportion of an industry's output or employment controlled by the five top enterprises, C_5, depends on the growth of large enterprises relative to the growth of smaller enterprises. This relative growth is partly determined by systematic or deterministic forces such as mergers or changes in optimum size of plant, and partly by stochastic or chance forces. By assumption, each of the latter effects is small and is independent of all the other forces and independent of the size of enterprise. There are so many of these stochastic shocks, some increasing and some decreasing the size of an enterprise, that it is impossible to enumerate them. If it were possible to specify any one significant stochastic force influencing the size of an enterprise, it could be included among the systematic factors influencing growth.

An example will help to clarify the distinction between the systematic and the stochastic or chance forces. In industry A the share of the five top enterprises in total output increases because each of the five acquires a smaller firm. In industry B the value of C_5 increases by the same amount as in industry A, but from entirely different causes; new enterprises enter the ranks of the top five for a multitude of reasons, including making correct economic forecasts of required output, reorganising production schedules to increase efficiency, being unaffected by shortages of components brought about by strikes in a component manufacturer which usually supplies the previous members of the top five . . . the list of possible reasons is endless. In the next period the stochastic forces operating in industry B change direction and restore the former leaders to their dominant position, and C_5 may increase again. Clearly, the type of increase in concentration in industry B is quite different from the systematic and steady increase brought about by mergers in industry A.

Some writers, following Gibrat,[1] have suggested that the growth of enterprises is entirely stochastic and that the size distribution of enterprises, and hence the relative importance of the top five, is the result of a series of multiplicative random shocks which influence the size of a firm but which are independent of its size. That is, a large firm stands just as much chance as a small firm of increasing its size by p per cent. With this method of growth, usually called Gibrat's 'law of proportionate effect', the degree of concentration increases continuously over time purely as the result of stochastic forces.

While this purely stochastic theory provides useful insights into the relative growths of firms, and is thus a useful aid to understanding the reasons for increases in concentration, it does not pretend to be wholly adequate; systematic forces making for changes in concentration can be observed which need to be measured, and which supplement the stochastic forces. Consequently, we do not examine those aspects considered by

[1] R. Gibrat, *Les Inégalités Economiques*, Paris, Sirev, 1931.

Gibrat in the present volume: stochastic factors are important and they are neglected by the traditional neoclassical microeconomic theory, but this does not mean that everything else should be ignored.

Our first task is to measure the growth of industrial concentration. Chapter 2 investigates the growth in average industrial concentration, using data at the MLH level of aggregation over the period 1935–73. Data for 1975 became available after the completion of this study and, as shown by the summary in appendix 2E, these latest estimates do not alter our conclusions based on earlier figures. Although much of the technical discussion of the sources and methods used is consigned to appendices, the analysis in chapter 2 is sufficiently detailed to reveal the different rates of growth of average industrial concentration in five sub-periods within the 38-year period 1935–73. This long-run analysis is made possible by estimating new concentration ratios for 1958, 1963 and 1968. The growth of average concentration at the industry level is compared in chart 1.1 with the changes in the share of the hundred largest enterprises in total manufacturing net output estimated by Prais[1] and with the trend in industrial concentration at the four-digit level in the United States estimated by Mueller and Hamm.[2]

The Census of Production has also published concentration ratios for main *product groups* (not industries) for 1958, 1963, 1968 and 1975. These product groups are closer approximations to markets than are the industries and merit the separate study provided in chapter 3. Whilst information at the product level is available for a shorter time period than that for industries, for the years since 1958 when both sets of data are available, similar trends in average concentration are observed, as shown in chart 1.1. This is not to say, however, that industry and product concentration data are perfect substitutes. For example, as explained in appendix 3C, an analysis of concentration trends by broad industry groups reveals somewhat different pictures using product and industry concentration data over the period 1958–68. These discrepancies arise partly from differences in the generation of the data and partly from the different samples employed, and hence provide further justification for the separate analysis of product concentration in chapter 3.

The curves of chart 1.1 show a large increase in United Kingdom concentration in the period 1935–75. This contrasts markedly with United States experience, depicted in curve (5), of practically stable concentration

[1] Prais, *Evolution of Giant Firms*.
[2] W. F. Mueller and L. G. Hamm, 'Trends in industrial market concentration 1947 to 1970', *Review of Economics and Statistics*, vol. 56, 1974.

Chart 1.1. *Trends in concentration since 1935*

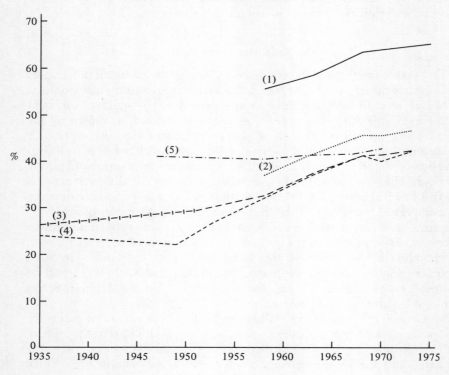

KEY
(1) Equally weighted mean C_5s for 144 products (1958–68) and 256 products (1968–75).
(2) Equally weighted mean C_5s for 79 industries (1973: 74 industries only).
(3) Equally weighted mean C_3s for 42 industries (1970 and 1973: 40 industries only). The 1935–51 trend is based on results from other samples described in chapter 2.
(4) Share of 100 top UK firms in manufacturing net output.
(5) Equally weighted mean C_4s for 166 US industries.
SOURCES: Chapters 2 and 3; Prais, *Evolution of Giant Firms*; Mueller and Hamm, 'Trends in industrial market concentration'.

levels from 1947 to 1970. Broadly speaking, United Kingdom trends divide into three. Prior to 1958 concentration increased at a moderate rate from 1951 to 1958, and probably at a somewhat slower rate from 1935 to 1951 as shown by curve (3). The slight upward movement in three-enterprise employment concentration in 1935–51, contrasts with a slight fall in the share of the hundred largest enterprises in manufacturing net output as a whole in 1935–49 shown in curve (4). This discrepancy can perhaps be explained by the slight difference in time period, although it is possible that wartime and postwar controls on the very largest firms may have affected the aggregate concentration measure. The limitations of the data available for this early period should make us careful not to place too much emphasis on this apparent discrepancy.

The period 1958–68 saw a marked acceleration in the rate of increase in market concentration. The average share of the five largest enterprises in the sales of products increased from 55.4 per cent in 1958 to 63.4 per cent in 1968 as shown by curve (1). The average share of the five largest enterprises in the employment of more broadly defined MLHs in curve (2) showed a similar increase from 36.9 per cent in 1958 to 45.6 per cent in 1968. Despite the differences between these two measures which are discussed in chapters 2 and 3 below, the general conformity of these trends justifies the use of industry concentration ratios to examine the causes and effects of concentration.

Finally, concentration at industry level after 1968 shows a deceleration in the rate of increase. Changes in the coverage of the Census of Production for 1970, which tended to reduce average levels of concentration, probably account for the slight fall between 1968 and 1970. But subsequent census data for 1970–5 reveal that the long-term upward trend in average industrial concentration, measured by the average share of the five largest enterprises in the employment of each industry, decelerated in the early 1970s. This finding is confirmed using the most recent product concentration data for 1968–75 in curve (1), where the average share of the five largest enterprises in the sales of products increased from 63.4 per cent in 1968 to 65.1 per cent in 1975 in a comparable sample of 256 products. The available evidence suggests that the rate of concentration increase fell back to 1950s levels in the early 1970s, emphasising again the dramatic nature of the concentration increases in the period 1958–68. Possible explanations for these increases are examined in some detail in chapters 4 and 5.

An econometric analysis of the causes of the growth of industrial concentration is provided in chapter 4. A similar econometric analysis is not possible for products, so chapter 5 adopts a descriptive approach, based on the case studies in our interim report,[1] to the assessment of the causes of increases and decreases in product concentration. These case studies reveal a number of other factors which are important in producing concentration change and which it was not possible to quantify in chapter 4. If they were asked to specify the most important causes of the average increase in industrial and product concentration, most people would put mergers and economies of scale at the top of their lists. There is some justification for this view, but chapter 4 shows that these systematic factors have less effect on the increase in industrial concentration than is commonly supposed. Although plant economies of scale are closely associated with the *level* of

---

[1] Hart, Utton and Walshe, *Mergers and Concentration in British Industry*.

industrial concentration, they explain only a very small part of the *increase*
in concentration over the decade 1958–68. Again, our statistical analysis
shows that mergers explained only a small part of the variation between
industries of proportionate concentration changes over the period
1958–68. This result is probably attributable in part to problems involved
in the measurement of expenditure on mergers at industry level. Indeed
the case studies summarised in chapter 5 suggest that mergers had a
substantial effect in increasing the average level of product concentration
and we prefer this result, even though the sample of products is
considerably smaller than the sample of industries used in the statistical
analyses of chapter 4. For the other significant systematic variables data
are available at industry level and the statistical results are more robust;
while plant economies of scale (but not advertising expenditure) tend to
increase industrial concentration, the growth of an industry and a high
initial concentration level tend to reduce it. Even so, the variation in
proportionate changes in industrial concentration attributable to all these
systematic factors together is not large, so that other factors must also be at
work.

This residual variation confirms the view that a stochastic model based
on the inherent variability of firms' profitability and growth rates, such as
that of Gibrat or of Galton, may be used to analyse changes in
concentration. Such an approach would have the advantage of stressing
dynamic factors at work which make changes in industrial concentration a
far more complex process than is envisaged in the simple theories of
continually increasing industrial concentration brought about by increasing economies of scale and mergers. It is true that some elementary
stochastic models, such as that of Gibrat, imply continually increasing
industrial concentration, but other models, such as that of Galton, do not
imply this and could be adapted very easily. Nevertheless, in spite of the
attractions of such models, they are not used here; instead we explore the
complex causes of changes in concentration at a more basic level, using the
case studies. These show that economies of scale and mergers contributed
to increasing product concentration in some cases, but other forces acting
in this direction were forward integration policies, market contraction, and
various government measures such as those embodied in the Restrictive
Trade Practices Act and in the Industrial Reorganisation Corporation. On
the other hand, product concentration was decreased by market growth,
by low entry barriers, by high initial levels of concentration, and by
limitations on the acquisition of enterprises. These findings emerge from
the samples of products used, but it is not possible to use statistical
techniques to generalise these results to all industrial products.

However, we can use statistical techniques to measure the persistence of
the increase (or decrease) in concentration. A regression of the changes in

industrial concentration ratios from 1963 to 1968 on those from 1958 to 1963 showed that the serial correlation coefficient was not significantly different from zero. Again, similar regressions for 144 comparable products 1958–63–68, and 222 comparable products 1963–68–75, yielded coefficients which were not significantly different from zero. That is, there was no tendency for individual industries or products with increases in concentration in the earlier period to have an increase in the second period, even though *on average* concentration increased in both periods, as shown in chapters 2 and 3.

Thus the continuous increase in average product concentration masks a turmoil of increases and decreases in the concentration ratios of individual industries and products. The upshot is that, although some systematic causes of increases in concentration such as mergers are important, the mass of stochastic factors influencing concentration are also important. The latter differ from industry to industry and from product to product, and explain the need for individual case studies in addition to standard regression analyses which merely measure *average* tendencies. The case studies also reveal the identities of the five top enterprises and show how their rank order changes over time. These changes indicate a degree of competition which is hidden by a concentration ratio and provide another reason for undertaking case studies.[1]

The economic effects of the growth of industrial concentration, which may be interpreted as an increase in the average degree of oligopoly in British industries, are considered in chapter 6. Was this increase associated with a faster increase in prices or in price–cost margins? Was it associated with higher wages? One would expect trade unions to ensure that their members enjoyed a share of any excess profits. Did this decrease in competition affect efficiency? Some commentators claim that monopoly breeds inefficiency while others claim that it leads to increased efficiency. These questions raise important issues of economic policy and chapter 6 answers each in turn.

Briefly, there is no evidence for the periods 1958–63 and 1963–8 to support the view that increases in industrial concentration tend to produce increases in prices. The main determinants of the variations of price increases between industries were variations in labour productivity and in raw-material prices. Variations in wage increases between industries were

---

[1] It is possible to use standard statistical techniques to measure the size mobility of enterprises, or the associated changes in rank order, provided that data on individual enterprises are available, as shown by Hart and Prais, 'The analysis of business concentration'. The same techniques were applied to firms in the brewing industry (P. E. Hart, 'On measuring business concentration', *Bulletin of the Oxford University Institute of Statistics*, vol. 19, 1957). We are unable to use these statistical techniques in the present study because we do not have census data on individual enterprises. Were the required figures available, they would probably emphasise the turmoil which underlies the steady increase in average industrial concentration.

too small to produce a significant effect on the variation of price increases, though of course *average* wage increases played an important part in the average increase in prices in the manufacturing industries studied.

Nor is there any evidence to justify the belief that changes in concentration are generally associated with changes in price–cost margins. There is some evidence, however, which suggests that labour absorbs a small part of the potential excess profits of oligopoly which arise in standard economic theories; but there is no statistical evidence to show that any part of these excess profits is absorbed by technical inefficiency. The absence of such general tendencies does not imply that there are no cases where oligopoly breeds higher prices, higher profitability and possibly less efficiency. It simply means that each oligopoly must be examined in the traditional British case-by-case approach to ensure that such abuses of oligopoly power do not occur.

Finally, chapter 7 summarises the discussion and is followed by a series of appendices which describe the statistical sources and methods which underpin our work. In addition, more specialised appendices, including those on the underlying theoretical models, are available separately in the National Institute Discussion Paper series, as noted in the List of Contents.

2

THE GROWTH OF CONCENTRATION AT INDUSTRY LEVEL

INTRODUCTION

There have been several important studies of concentration at the industry level since 1945 when Leak and Maizels published the first British concentration ratios for 1935. The study by Evely and Little[1] provided industrial concentration ratios for 1951, which in turn were compared with some of the 1958 Census of Production industrial concentration ratios by Armstrong and Silberston[2] and by Shepherd.[3] The period 1958–63 was further considered by Sawyer,[4] who estimated minimum and maximum four-firm concentration ratios for 1958 and 1963. The present chapter extends the series to 1973 by deriving new sets of concentration ratios from size distributions of enterprises by employment for 1958, 1963 and 1968, and by using concentration ratios published in the annual Censuses of Production since 1970.[5] These extensions permit the examination of long-term trends in concentration at the industry level.

The trends in concentration at this level must be distinguished from the trend in aggregate business concentration, measured for example by the changing share of the hundred largest enterprises in total net output in manufacturing, which was investigated by Prais.[6] Concentration ratios at the industry (three-digit) level are obviously closer to the economists' concept of the degree of monopoly than is the share of the hundred largest enterprises in manufacturing industry as a whole. Even so, the Census of Production industry used here, which is defined in terms of a group of principal products 'commonly associated in production' and 'usually similar in nature or manner of production',[7] is not in practice always closely related to the economists' definition of an industry as a group of products with high cross price-elasticities of demand and supply; most

[1] Evely and Little, *Concentration in British Industry.*
[2] A. Armstrong and A. Silberston, 'Size of plant, size of enterprise and concentration in British manufacturing industry 1935–58', *Journal of the Royal Statistical Society* (series A), vol. 128, part 3, 1965.
[3] W. G. Shepherd, 'Changes in British industrial concentration 1951–1958', *Oxford Economic Papers*, vol. 18, 1966.
[4] M. C. Sawyer, 'Concentration in British manufacturing industry', *Oxford Economic Papers*, vol. 23, 1971.
[5] Appendix 2E summarises the recently published data for 1975.
[6] Prais, *Evolution of Giant Firms.*
[7] *Report on the Census of Production 1968*, part 1 : *Description of the Census*, p. 16.

11

notably because the census definition sometimes ignores the demand side. From some points of view concentration ratios at the product (four-digit) level are even closer approximations to the economists' concept of the degree of monopoly and an analysis of such ratios is presented in chapter 3. It was, however, shown in chart 1.1 that for the period 1958 to 1968 when product and industry concentration data overlap similar trends are observed, and this supports the use of industry concentration data in this chapter to outline long-term concentration trends.

The type of question posed and answered in this chapter takes the form: 'did the average degree of concentration in manufacturing industry increase between 1935 and 1973, and if so, at what rate?' Answers are provided in each of the sections of this chapter dealing with the sub-periods 1935–51, 1951–8, 1958–68 and 1968–73. Samples of industries distributed by values of their employment concentration ratios and the means of these distributions, with equal weights for each industry and with industry employment weights, are used in formulating these answers.[1]

It must be stressed that these samples are not random but are simply the largest number of comparable industries which could be obtained for any one period. It could be argued that the exclusion of industries which enter or leave the Census of Production or which are redefined, means that old, declining industries and new, expanding industries are not allowed to affect the measurement of long-term trends in average concentration; yet such industries are likely to have substantial changes in concentration. Our implicit hypothesis is that the likely increase in concentration in old declining industries is offset by the likely decrease in concentration in new expanding industries. By definition, concentration ratios for such industries are not available for both the initial and terminal years of each period studied and there is no way of testing our hypothesis. However, some indication of the extent to which the samples are representative is given in appendix 2D, which classifies the concentration data by Industrial Orders.

In addition to specifying the Industrial Orders where the concentration data have strong or weak representation, appendix 2D highlights those sectors with extreme changes in concentration which are not revealed by the changes in average industrial concentration considered in this chapter. For example, there was an outstanding increase in industrial concentration in Order III (food, drink and tobacco) in 1958–63, following the largest increase in 1951–8.

The estimation of industrial concentration ratios for 1958, 1963 and 1968 is described in appendix 2C, while appendix 2B describes the selection of the samples of comparable industries. Appendix 2A summarises the relationships between average concentration ratios with different weights.

[1] Frequency distributions have been compiled and are available on request from the authors.

THE PERIOD 1935-51

This is the earliest period for which industrial concentration data are available, but we shall deal with it fairly quickly for two reasons. First, the period was one of economic disruption caused by war and postwar controls, so that only limited significance can be placed on a comparison of market structure in 1951 with market structure in 1935. By observing these two end-years we can determine the net change in concentration over the whole period, but it may be that this tells us little either about concentration trends within the period or about the broader secular trends in which we are interested. Secondly, the subject has already been treated in some detail by Evely and Little[1] and we do not propose to do more than reinforce the conclusions usually drawn from their work.

These conclusions are, in brief, that there was some evidence of an increase in concentration between 1935 and 1951, but that the increase was small. Such conclusions may be drawn from a comparison of the three-firm employment concentration means for Leak and Maizels'[2] central sample of 249 trades and sub-trades in 1935 and Evely and Little's central sample of 220 trades and sub-trades in 1951. Using employment weights, these showed values of 26 per cent and 29 per cent respectively, suggesting that, on average over the sixteen-year period, concentration increased by about 0.2 percentage points per annum. Evely and Little were, however, more cautious in drawing conclusions from these results. Being conscious of the limitations of the data, they refrained from drawing any general conclusions on the change in concentration over the period. In their view 'it is impossible to come to any definite and clear-cut conclusion about the change in the level of concentration in British industry between 1935 and 1951'.[3] Instead they proceeded 'on a selective rather than a general basis', choosing to examine concentration changes between 1935 and 1951 through a sample of 41 trades and sub-trades for which a definite change in principal product concentration could be identified.[4]

Hart, Utton and Walshe took the mid-points of the interval estimates of principal product concentration for these 41 trades and sub-trades, and regressed 1951 concentration on 1935 concentration, showing that there was hardly any tendency for low-concentration trades to increase their concentration more quickly than the high-concentration trades.[5] In this

[1] Evely and Little, *Concentration in British Industry*.
[2] Leak and Maizels, 'The structure of British industry'.
[3] Evely and Little, *Concentration in British Industry*, p. 63.
[4] For full details of their methods of selection of this sample, see *ibid*, chapter X. A list of these trades, together with interval estimates of principal product concentration ratios, can be found in their table 29, p. 152; whilst the method of calculating these interval estimates is given in their appendix D.
[5] Hart, Utton and Walshe, *Mergers and Concentration*, table 3, p. 29. As an example of the interval estimates of C_3 made by Evely and Little, table 29, p. 152, we may cite cement, which had a C_3 of 68–79 in 1935 and 79–89 in 1951.

regression the use of the Evely and Little sample may be justified, because by giving more weight to the larger and more certain changes in concentration, one is less likely to bias the estimate of the regression slope. For the purpose of estimating the average change in concentration of all industries, however, this sample may be inappropriate. The major criterion for the selection of the sample was that interval estimates of principal product concentration should not overlap. This inevitably meant that trades with small and uncertain concentration changes tended to be excluded. Thus the increase from 42.0 per cent in 1935 to 51.5 per cent in 1951 in the equally weighted mean concentration ratio for this sample of 41 comparable trades may not have been representative of all the trades.

As noted by Evely and Little it is extremely difficult to select a representative sample of comparable trades and sub-trades for the period 1935 to 1951. Nevertheless, we have selected 98 such trades and sub-trades, as explained in appendix 2B, in order to make such a comparison. These trades and sub-trades represent 40 per cent of employment in manufacturing and mining in 1951, compared with the 9 per cent of employment in all trades in 1951 accounted for by Evely and Little's 41 trades and sub-trades. Equally weighted and employment-weighted concentration ratios for these trades are shown in table 2.1.

It is possible for different measures of central tendency of the distribution of trades by concentration ratio to yield different estimates of the amount or even the direction of change in C_3. In the present work, four measures of central tendency are used, namely the arithmetic mean with equal, initial-year, terminal-year, and current-year weights. Table 2.1

Table 2.1. *Equally weighted and employment-weighted mean C_3 for 98 comparable trades and sub-trades, 1935 and 1951*

Percentages

	1935	1951	Change in C_3 1935–51		
			In mean	In weights	Total
Equal weights	34.9	38.3	3.4	—	3.4
Employment weights					
1935	23.9	26.1	2.2	1.4	3.6[a]
1951	25.8	27.5	1.7	1.9	3.6[a]

SOURCES: Leak and Maizels, 'The structure of British industry', appendix III; Evely and Little, *Concentration in British Industry*, appendices B and J; appendix 2B below.
[a] At current weights, i.e. change in mean C_3 using current weights is 27.5–23.9 = 3.6.

shows that with equal weights it increased from 34.9 per cent in 1935 to 38.3 per cent in 1951, corresponding to an increase on average of about 0.2 percentage points per annum. This rate of increase is confirmed when current-year employment weights are used, since $27.5 - 23.9 = 3.6$ is similar to the 3.4 percentage point increase in the equally weighted mean. However, when initial-year and terminal-year weights are used the increases are smaller, being 2.2 and 1.7 percentage points respectively. That is, if the distribution of employment between industries in 1935 had persisted until 1951, average concentration would have increased by 2.2 percentage points. The difference of 1.4 points between this increase and the increase of 3.6 points in the current-weighted mean is attributable to the effects of changes in weights, which in this instance imply that employment in the more concentrated industries tended to increase relatively to employment in the less concentrated industries. This is shown in the changes in C_3 in table 2.1, or more formally in appendix 2A. If we use 1951 weights the effects of changes in weights become more important than the change in average concentration. The broad conclusion must be that over the period 1935–51 the increase in average industrial concentration must be attributed to two approximately equal forces: the tendency for industries to become more concentrated, and the tendency of the more concentrated industries to expand relatively to the others. However, the annual rate of increase in average concentration was relatively small over this period, whatever measure is used.[1]

The level of employment concentration for this sample of trades and sub-trades in 1951 was 38.3 per cent measured by the equally weighted mean and 27.5 per cent measured by the 1951 employment-weighted mean. The absolute levels observed have limited significance since they depend on the ratio of sub-trades to trades in the sample, with the more disaggregated sub-trades having higher concentration ratios on average. More important is the fact that the equally weighted mean is 10 percentage points above the employment-weighted mean. This indicates, as noted by Evely and Little, that in 1951 there was a negative correlation of trade size and concentration ratio, as explained in appendix 2A. Thus in 1951, 43 trades and sub-trades were relatively competitive in structure (with C_3 less than 30 per cent), but these 44 per cent of trades and sub-trades accounted for 65 per cent of employment in the sample. At the other end of the scale, there were ten relatively concentrated trades (with C_3 over 70 per cent) in 1951, which accounted for only 4 per cent of employment in the sample.

---

[1] These results were also confirmed in a comparison of net output and gross output concentration ratios for this sample of trades and sub-trades over the period, as well as in various other (non-comparable) samples used. In no case was a fall in concentration observed in the period 1935–51, and most cases showed a small rise. See also S. Aaronovitch and M. C. Sawyer, *Big Business: Theoretical and Empirical Aspects of Concentration and Mergers in the United Kingdom*, London, Macmillan, 1975, pp. 16–17, who found using different (non-comparable) samples a rise in employment-weighted mean C_3 from 29.1 per cent in 1935 to 31.2 per cent in 1951.

THE PERIOD 1951–8

Industry concentration trends in the period 1951–8 can be examined by comparing the three-enterprise concentration ratios provided for 1951 by Evely and Little[1] with the 1958 sales, net output and employment concentration ratios provided in Summary Table 5 of the 1958 Census of Production. In addition, in table 3 of the individual census reports on each industry, there are size distributions of enterprises by employment which can also be used to estimate 1958 employment concentration ratios. Unfortunately, the data available for the period suffer from two shortcomings. First, there was a change in the SIC in 1958 resulting in a considerable reclassification of industries, which severely restricts the number of comparable industries over the period. Secondly, there was a less consistent use of three-enterprise concentration ratios, C_3, in the 1958 Census than in 1951. Of the 125 industries for which concentration ratios are available in Summary Table 5 of the 1958 Census, only 58 relate to the three largest enterprises, the rest relating to more.

In their excellent study of the period, Armstrong and Silberston found that only 63 manufacturing industries were reasonably comparable in 1951–8.[2] As they noted, these industries tend to be smaller than average, covering 52.5 per cent of manufacturing industries, but only 40 per cent of their gross output or employment in 1958. Furthermore, engineering industries were particularly affected by census reclassification, and so are poorly represented in their sample of 63 industries. Their sample of industries was, therefore, not random and this should be borne in mind in considering their results, as well as the results using a similar sample of 57 industries reported below.

Their solution to the problem of too few values of C_3 was to compute maximum and minimum possible values of C_3 from values of Cr $(r > 3)$ for 1958 as explained in their appendix 2D. This procedure enabled them to determine the direction of change in three-enterprise employment concentration in 54 industries. They found that it increased in 36 industries, while in eighteen industries there was a decrease or no change. This result was corroborated by Shepherd, who also found a 2:1 ratio in favour of concentration increases in the period.[3] These findings establish a prima facie case for Armstrong and Silberston's general conclusion that 'the extent to which many industries are dominated by a few "giant"

---

[1] Evely and Little, *Concentration in British Industry*.

[2] These industries are listed in Armstrong and Silberston, 'Size of plant, size of enterprise and concentration', table 6, pp. 418–19. In fact, some of these industries were also affected to some extent by reclassification: particularly bread and flour confectionery, and animal and poultry foods.

[3] Shepherd, 'Changes in British industrial concentration'. He succeeded in matching 73 manufacturing industries in the period, finding that 49 had increases and 24 had decreases or no change in concentration.

enterprises seems to be increasing'.[1] The proportion of industries with concentration rises in 1951–8 is similar to the proportion found by Evely and Little in their sample of 41 industries for 1935–51,[2] although the latter period is considerably longer.

Armstrong and Silberston made no attempt to measure the average increase in concentration in the period. Such an attempt is made here for employment C_3 in table 2.2 using 57 comparable industries over the

Table 2.2. *Equally weighted and employment-weighted mean C_3 for 57 comparable industries, 1951 and 1958*

Percentages

	1951	1958	Change in C_3 1951–8		
			In mean	In weights	Total
Equal weights	31.2	33.9	2.7	—	2.7
Employment weights					
1951	23.2	25.7	2.5	1.1	3.6[a]
1958	24.9	26.8	1.9	1.7	3.6[a]

sources: Evely and Little, *Concentration in British Industry*, appendix B; Armstrong and Silberston, 'Size of plant, size of enterprise and concentration'; appendices 2B and 2C below.
[a] At current weights as in table 2.1.

period, as explained in appendix 2B to this chapter.[3] In order to derive quantitative estimates of the change in concentration in 1951–8, enterprise size distributions for each industry in 1958 were used to construct industry concentration curves from which C_3, when not given in the distribution, was estimated by extrapolation as explained in appendix 2C. As noted there, estimates of the share of employment accounted for by the three largest enterprises are subject to a larger margin of error than the estimates of C_5 which are used in the next section of this chapter. Nevertheless, the usefulness of such estimates in enabling us to measure the change in concentration in the period was thought to justify the attempt. In addition, an analysis of 29 of the 57 industries for which C_3 was given exactly in 1958 produced very similar conclusions to those given in table 2.2. Whilst therefore our results should be treated with caution, we are reasonably confident that they are reliable.

The 57 comparable industries of table 2.2 represented 37 per cent of employment in United Kingdom manufacturing and mining (excluding

[1] Shepherd reached a similar conclusion from his comparable sample of 73 industries, and also from a non-comparable sample of all manufacturing industries in 1951 and 1958. His calculations were in terms of net output concentration.
[2] Evely and Little, *Concentration in British Industry* (table 29, p. 152), found that 27 industries had concentration rises and 14 had falls in their sample of 41 industries.
[3] The employment concentration ratios for 1951 have been adjusted to cover all firms. Armstrong and Silberston adjusted their 1958 ratios to exclude firms with ten or less employees ('Size of plant, size of enterprise and concentration', table 6, pp. 418–19).

coal mines) in 1958. Inspection of the equally weighted mean C_3 reveals that concentration increased from 31.2 per cent in 1951 to 33.9 per cent in 1958. This increase of 2.7 percentage points is slightly larger than that observed using constant-employment weights, but smaller than the increase from 23.2 per cent in 1951 to 26.8 per cent in 1958 using current-year employment weights. As for the period 1935–51, each measure indicates an increase in concentration in the period 1951 to 1958 and, moreover, the absolute magnitudes of change are much the same for both periods. This implies that the rate of concentration increase accelerated in the period 1951–8, for that period was only seven years compared with the sixteen between 1935 and 1951. On average in the period 1951 to 1958 concentration increased by about 0.4 percentage points per annum compared with the 0.2 percentage points per annum observed from 1935 to 1951. These results confirm the view implicit in the work of Armstrong and Silberston, and of Shepherd, that the rate of concentration increase speeded up in United Kingdom manufacturing industry in the 1950s.

The change in the current-weighted mean C_3 is also given in table 2.2. It can be seen that with both 1951 and 1958 weights the increase in average concentration was more important than the tendency for the more highly concentrated industries to increase their employment relative to others. Nevertheless, the effects of the changes in weights, were responsible for between 30 and 47 per cent of the increase of 3.6 points in the current-weighted mean.

THE PERIOD 1958–68

The data for the measurement of industrial concentration in the decade 1958–68 were compiled from size distributions of enterprises given in the Census of Production for the years 1958, 1963 and 1968, as described in detail in appendix 2C. In this section it was decided to use employment concentration ratios for the five largest enterprises, C_5, since at this level the margin for error in the estimates was typically small, and certainly smaller than in estimates of C_4 or C_3. Each of the sub-periods 1958–63 and 1963–8, as well as 1958–68, is examined. A similar approach is used in chapter 3 in discussing trends in product concentration over these same years.

1958–63
Industry concentration in the sub-period 1958–63 has been investigated by Sawyer, who used four-enterprise employment concentration ratios (C_4) for 117 manufacturing industries.[1] He calculated minimum and

[1] Sawyer, 'Concentration in British manufacturing industry'. His calculations are in his appendix II and the method of their derivation in his appendix III.

maximum possible ratios for each industry for each year and, using the simple average of these, he found that the weighted average $C4$ increased from 29.0 per cent in 1958 to 32.2 per cent in 1963. Similar rises in concentration were also found for $C8$, $C12$ and $C20$, which is important because cumulative concentration curves can cross.[1] It was possible to be confident about the direction of concentration change in the period at a level below $C16$ in all but one of the industries (bolts, nuts, screws, rivets, etc.). Sawyer found that 91 industries increased in concentration, while thirteen decreased, and twelve had concentration curves which crossed. At the $C4$ level a definite result was available in 76 cases, although in nine of these the concentration curves crossed elsewhere. Of the remaining 67 industries, 62 had concentration increases, and only five decreases. These and other indicators led Sawyer to conclude that 'the level of concentration in the manufacturing sector of British industry has increased over the years 1958–63'.[2]

Whilst not questioning Sawyer's general conclusion, it remains true that his method of simply averaging minimum and maximum possible four-enterprise concentration ratios is somewhat arbitrary. As indicated in appendix 2C this procedure is particularly sensitive to the amount of information available for calculating the bounds of four-enterprise concentration in each of the years. Our own method of estimation described in appendix 2C may also be subject to error, but on the whole it should provide a more accurate description of concentration changes in the period 1958–63; this justifies a re-examination of the average concentration change in the period. Our point estimates were used to examine the average change in concentration in a sample of 119 industries representing 97 per cent of 1963 employment in United Kingdom manufacturing and mining (excluding coal mines).[3]

Equally weighted and employment-weighted mean concentration ratios for those 119 industries are given in table 2.3. The equally weighted mean increased by 4.3 percentage points from 38.4 per cent in 1958 to 42.7 per cent in 1963. The current-year employment-weighted mean increased by 4.5 percentage points (or 14 per cent) from 32.6 per cent in 1958 to 37.1 per cent in 1963. Slightly larger increases were observed when constant-employment weights were used. These increases are a shade larger than the 3.2 points rise (or 11 per cent) found by Sawyer using four-firm weighted mean employment concentration ratios. Sawyer's simple method, though showing the correct direction, seems to have understated the size of the change. In addition, the average increase appears to be much larger than that observed in 1951–8, and *a fortiori* larger than that

---

[1] *Ibid.* p. 355.
[2] *Ibid.* p. 374.
[3] The sample is described in appendix 2B, and our point estimates of $C5$ are given in table 2C.1.

Table 2.3. *Equally weighted and employment-weighted mean C5 for 119 comparable industries, 1958 and 1963*

Percentages

	1958	1963	Change in C_5 1958–63		
			In mean	In weights	Total
Equal weights	38.4	42.7	4.3	—	4.3
Employment weights					
1958	32.6	37.7	5.1	−0.6	4.5[a]
1963	32.4	37.1	4.7	−0.2	4.5[a]

SOURCES: See appendices 2B and 2C.

[a] At current weights as in table 2.1.

observed in 1935–51. Moreover, 94 of the 119 industries had increases in C_5 in this period, which was a higher proportion than the two thirds observed in 1951–8. This finding also lends support to the conclusion that the increase in industry concentration further accelerated in 1958–63.[1] Furthermore, the increase of 4.5 points in the current-weighted mean was primarily due to the increase in average concentration, as shown in table 2.3. In contrast with the tendency for employment to be redistributed towards the more highly concentrated industries up to 1958, the change in employment weights in 1958–63 had the opposite effect of slightly *reducing* average concentration.

1963–8

For the sub-period 1963–8, 149 industries in manufacturing and mining were specified by the 1968 Census, of which twelve are excluded from the present section for reasons given in appendix 2B. The 137 remaining industries accounted for 89.5 per cent of employment in United Kingdom manufacturing and mining (excluding coal mining) in 1968, and the mean concentration ratios are presented in table 2.4. The equally weighted mean increased by 2.9 percentage points from 44.9 per cent in 1963 to 47.8 per cent in 1968. The current-year employment-weighted mean increased by 3.9 percentage points from 39.7 per cent in 1963 to 43.6 per cent in 1968. Clearly, mean industrial concentration continued to increase over the period 1963 to 1968 whether measured by equally or unequally weighted means. These rises are slightly lower than those recorded for the 119 industries in 1958–63, a result which contrasts with the finding at the

[1] This finding contrasts with the view expressed in a recent government Green Paper (Department of Prices and Consumer Protection, *A Review of Monopolies and Mergers Policy*, Cmnd 7198, London, HMSO, 1978) that concentration rises continued at a slower rate in 1958–63 (*ibid.* annex A, para. 28, p. 51). The view that concentration declined in 1935–51 (*ibid.* annex A, para. 26, p. 50) also contrasts with our findings reported above.

product level in chapter 3 that concentration increased slightly faster in 1963–8. However, it will be shown below that the differences, as in the product case, may be regarded as not statistically significant. Once again, changes in employment between industries had a slight negative effect on average concentration as shown in table 2.4.

Table 2.4. *Equally weighted and employment-weighted mean C5 for 137 comparable industries, 1963 and 1968*

Percentages

| | 1963 | 1968 | Change in C_5 1963–8 | | |
			In mean	In weights	Total
Equal weights	44.9	47.8	2.9	—	2.9
Employment weights					
1963	39.7	43.8	4.1	−0.2	3.9[a]
1968	39.6	43.6	4.0	−0.1	3.9[a]

SOURCES: See appendices 2B and 2C.

[a] At current weights as in table 2.1.

1958–68

In order to test whether the increase in mean concentration over the period 1958–63 was significantly different from the increase from 1963 to 1968, 79 industries were selected which were comparable throughout the decade 1958–68. The method of selection is described in appendix 2B. These industries account for just over half the number of industries specified in the 1968 Census and for 59 per cent of total employment in manufacturing and mining in 1968. The major reason the sample was so small was the increased number of industries in the 1968 Census which involved the breaking up or rearrangement of a number of industries separately specified in earlier Censuses, particularly among the chemicals and engineering groups. Other changes in 1968 also inhibited comparability, notably the treatment of parts as principal products in the mechanical engineering industry group in 1968, which effectively excluded all but two of the industries in this group.

Thus the 79 industries were not randomly selected; nor were they taken evenly from all branches of manufacturing and mining, as can be seen from appendix 2D. Metal manufacture is not represented at all, only three of the seventeen 1968 chemical industries are represented and only seven of the thirty 1968 engineering industries are included. On the other hand, textiles, bricks, pottery and glass, timber and furniture, and leather and fur are fully represented, while clothing and footwear is nearly so. This imbalance in the representation of 1968 Industrial Orders may affect the value of the results derived from this sample of 79 industries.

Table 2.5. *Equally weighted and employment-weighted mean C5 for 79 comparable industries, 1958, 1963 and 1968*

Percentages

	1958	1963^a	1968	Change in C5 1958–68			1963–8 minus 1958–63^c
				In mean	In weights	Total	
Equal weights	36.9	41.6	45.6	8.7	—	8.7	−0.7
Employment weights							
1958	33.8	39.3	44.6	10.8	0.2	11.0^b	−0.2
1963	34.0	39.6	44.7	..	..	..	−0.5
1968	34.2	39.7	44.8	10.6	0.4	11.0^b	−0.4

SOURCES: See appendices 2B and 2C.
^{a} Estimates for 1963 based on 1968 data source.
^{b} At current weights as in table 2.1.
^{c} Standard error is 0.9 in each case.

Table 2.5 provides equally weighted and employment-weighted mean concentration ratios for this sample of industries in 1958, 1963 and 1968. The equally weighted mean increased from 36.9 per cent in 1958 to 41.6 per cent in 1963 and 45.6 per cent in 1968. The employment-weighted means show slightly lower levels of concentration in each year, and slightly larger increases in each period. In all cases industry concentration increased slightly faster in the period 1958–63 than in 1963–8. However, employing a matched pairs test it was not possible to detect a significant difference between these increases at the 5 per cent level as indicated by the standard errors in table 2.5. Thus it would seem safest to conclude that concentration increased at much the same rate in both periods, a conclusion which is further supported in chapter 3 below, where trends in product concentration in a sample of 144 products in the period 1958–68 are examined.[1]

It is the acceleration in the rate of concentration increase in the period 1958–68 compared with the previous period 1951–8, rather than possible differences within the period 1958–68, which represents the most prominent feature of postwar concentration trends in United Kingdom manufacturing and mining. This is especially true when the effects of changes in weights are excluded. It can be seen from table 2.5 that nearly all of the change in average C5 at current weights between 1958 and 1968 was due to increases in concentration within industries. In fact the rate of increase was over 1 percentage point per annum. The corresponding

[1] For a contrary view, see, in particular, K. D. George, 'A note on changes in industrial concentration in the United Kingdom', *Economic Journal*, vol. 85, 1975, pp. 124–8 and *A Review of Monopolies and Mergers Policy*, Cmnd 7198, p. 51. This issue is discussed in more detail in chapter 3 below.

annual rates for 1935–51 and 1951–8 were about 0.12 and 0.3 percentage points respectively.

THE PERIOD SINCE 1968

The publication of concentration ratios in the annual Censuses of Production for 1970–3 enable us to consider the trend in concentration into the 1970s. Our original intention was to provide a further quinquennial estimate of average concentration trends for the period 1968–73. However, the change to annual Censuses in 1970, and the associated establishment of the new Central Production Register, is thought to have resulted in a fuller coverage of small firms in 1970 than in the 1968 Census. For this reason we have little confidence in the small fall in average concentration in 1968–70 observed in chart 1.1 and in this section we confine our analysis to concentration trends over the period 1970–3; although the period is very short, the available data are reasonably comparable.[1]

As explained in appendix 2B, it proved possible to select a comparable sample of 132 industries, representing 79 per cent of United Kingdom manufacturing and mining employment in 1973, over the three-year period 1970–3. Equally weighted and employment-weighted means for employment C_5 in 1970 and 1973 are given in table 2.6.[2] An inspection of the frequency distributions reveals a remarkable similarity between the

Table 2.6. *Equally weighted and employment-weighted mean C_5 for 132 comparable industries, 1970 and 1973*

Percentages

	1970	1973	Change in C_5 1970–3		
			In mean	In weights	Total
Equal weights	47.4	48.2	0.8	—	0.8
Employment weights					
1970	42.0	42.4	0.4	0.1	0.5[a]
1973	42.0	42.5	0.5	—	0.5[a]

SOURCES: See appendices 2B and 2C.
[a] At current weights as in table 2.1.

[1] Chart 1.1 indicates a slight fall in the equally weighted employment C_5 for the 79 industries found comparable 1958–68 from 45.6 per cent in 1968 to 45.4 per cent in 1970. A fuller comparison of 137 industries over the period reveals a fall from 47.3 per cent to 47.0 per cent using equal weights, and from 42.8 per cent to 42.2 per cent using current-year employment weights. For a preliminary analysis of the recently published 1975 data see appendix 2E.
[2] In 29 industries employment C_5 was estimated by the graphical method of appendix 2C. These cases involved more concentrated industries on average so that levels of concentration in table 2.6 are somewhat higher than if these industries are excluded. Employment concentration changes are much the same, however, with the exclusion of these industries, as indicated below.

distributions in the two years, although there is some evidence of concentration increase amongst industries with below-average concentration in 1970. As far as individual industries are concerned, 68 had concentration increases, while 49 had concentration falls, and fifteen had no change in concentration. This impression of only a slight increase in concentration over the period is borne out by inspection of the mean concentration ratios. These show a slight increase of 0.8 of a percentage point as measured by the equally weighted mean and 0.5 of a percentage point as measured by the current-year employment-weighted mean. These slight increases are not significantly different from zero at the 5 per cent significance level. Compared to an average increase in C_5 of close to 1.0 percentage points per annum in the period 1958–68, the evidence of table 2.6 suggests that there was a much less rapid concentration increase in the early 1970s. Table 2.6 also shows, in the analysis of the change in mean C_5, that there was little or no effect of changes in employment weights.

The predominant use of employment concentration ratios in this chapter was determined by the availability of data, although it has been indicated that, at least before 1958, net output and sales concentration trends conformed broadly to the pattern indicated by employment concentration. It is possible that employment concentration trends give a misleading impression of trends in net output and sales concentration in the period 1958–68, but it is not possible to test this proposition for that period. The publication of net output and sales concentration ratios in the annual Censuses since 1970, however, does allow us to investigate this possibility, albeit for the limited period 1970–3. Table 2.7 reports weighted and equally weighted mean concentration ratios for employment, sales and net output for 1970 and 1973 for a sample of 102 comparable industries.[1] In considering this table it should be noted that in all cases enterprises were ranked by employment, even when sales and net output concentration ratios were calculated. Hence levels of output concentration may be underestimated, and this may also affect the reported concentration trend using these output measures in the period 1970–3.

Table 2.7 in general supports the view that output concentration increased more sharply in the period than employment concentration. In all cases, sales concentration and net output concentration increased by more than employment concentration. Thus, for example, using 1973 weights, net output concentration increased by 0.6 percentage points per annum, compared with an increase in sales concentration of 0.5 points per annum and an increase in employment concentration of less than 0.1 points per annum. These findings therefore raise the possibility that the

[1] The sample of 102 comprises all those comparable industries for which C_5 was given exactly for employment, sales *and* net output in Summary Tables 9 and 11 of the 1970 and 1973 Census respectively.

Table 2.7. *Mean employment, sales and net output concentration for 102 industries,
1970 and 1973*

Percentages

	1970	1973	Change in C_5 1970–3		
			In mean	In weights	Total
Employment C_5					
Equal weights	42.8	43.3	0.5	—	0.5
1970 weights	39.5	39.6	0.1	0.1	0.2[a]
1973 weights	39.5	39.7	0.2	—	0.2[a]
Sales C_5					
Equal weights	43.6	45.4	1.8	—	1.8
1970 weights	43.7	45.3	1.6	—	1.6[a]
1973 weights	43.8	45.3	1.5	0.1	1.6[a]
Net output C_5					
Equal weights	43.9	45.7	1.8	—	1.8
1970 weights	42.6	43.8	1.2	0.1	1.3[a]
1973 weights	42.2	43.9	1.7	−0.4	1.3[a]

SOURCES: See text.
[a] At current weights as in table 2.1.

small rise in employment concentration gives a misleading picture of
concentration trends in the early 1970s. Unfortunately lack of data on sales
and net output concentration for the period 1958–68 makes it impossible to
compare the 1970–3 trend in output concentration with the earlier period.
It should be noted, however, that even the large rises in output
concentration in 1970–3 are well below the rises in employment
concentration reported for 1958–68.

Reasons for the discrepancy between trends in net output and sales
concentration on the one hand, and employment concentration on the
other, remain a matter of conjecture. The possibility that it arises from
shortcomings in the data, as already noted, cannot be ruled out. If one
accepts the results of table 2.7 at face value, however, it could be argued
that in the period larger firms in each industry were able to raise prices more
than all firms, an argument which finds support in economic theory.
Against this, however, is the impressionistic evidence that price controls,
in so far as these were important in this period, were particularly directed at
larger firms and would have tended to prevent this. On the other hand, it
might be that in the period leading firms in each industry tended to increase
their labour productivity faster than all firms, possibly because of their
ability to obtain more capital on easier terms. It may be that the figures
indicate that the much heralded rationalisation of production following
the merger boom of the 1960s did give rise to production efficiency gains in

the following years. These hypotheses must await further data and research before a firm conclusion can be drawn.

The finding that the rate of concentration increase, as measured by the employment concentration ratios, decelerated in the early 1970s compared with the 1960s is perhaps surprising, particularly since it is known that merger activity remained buoyant in the early 1970s. Figures on numbers and values of mergers are given in table 2.8. Peak years in terms of

Table 2.8. *Mergers of industrial and commercial companies, 1963–73*

	Number	Index of value [a]
1963	888	100
1964	940	134
1965	1000	146
1966	807	140
1967	763	216
1968	946	362
1969[b]	907	176
1969[b]	846	201
1970	793	238
1971	884	164
1972	1210	357
1973	1205	213

SOURCE: *A Review of Monopolies and Mergers Policy*, Cmnd 7198, appendix D, table 1.
[a] Consideration paid in current prices deflated by FT Actuaries 500 Ordinary Share Index.
[b] The series up to 1969 is based on company accounts; 1969 onwards on financial press and other sources.

numbers of mergers (over a thousand) were 1965, and 1972 and 1973, whilst in terms of value of consideration paid in real terms 1968 and 1972 stand out. Thus it is not possible to argue that the apparent deceleration in the rate of increase in concentration is attributable to a decline in gross merger activity in the early 1970s. On the other hand, evidence with respect to mergers vetted by the Mergers Panel,[1] indicates that after 1970 a marked decline in the proportion of horizontal mergers occurred, with 85 per cent or more of mergers being horizontal prior to 1970, but only roughly two thirds being horizontal thereafter. The principal reason for this change was the increased importance of conglomerate mergers from 1970 onwards and this finding is consistent with a less marked increase in industry concentration in the period 1970–3. It is argued in chapter 5, however, that whilst mergers play an important role in market concentration trends, they remain only part of the story. Thus we must be careful not to take an over-simplified view of the relationship between mergers and market concentration trends in the period 1970–3.

[1] *A Review of Monopolies and Mergers Policy*, Cmnd 7198, appendix D, table 5, p. 110.

CONCLUSIONS

The above investigations show that there has been a persistent tendency for average industrial concentration to increase in United Kingdom manufacturing and mining at least since 1951, and probably since 1935. This trend is summarised in table 2.9 and chart 1.1 by considering a comparable sample of 42 industries over the period 1951–73. Since it was required to go back to 1951, it was necessary to measure employment concentration at the three-enterprise level. Estimates of C_3 are less reliable than those of C_5, but the general conformity of concentration trends shown with our earlier findings justifies the exercise. Table 2.9 and chart 1.1 provide equally weighted mean C_3 estimates for the United Kingdom, which are compared with concentration ratios for the United States for the years 1947–70 estimated by Mueller and Hamm.[1] The 42 industries were selected by matching as many as possible of the 57 industries available for 1951–8 with the 79 industries available for 1958–68.

Table 2.9. *Comparison of concentration trends in 42 United Kingdom industries with 166 United States industries in the postwar period*

	UK C_3			US C_4	
Date	Level	Rate of change	Date	Level	Rate of change
	(%)	(% p.a.)		(%)	(% p.a.)
			1947	40.9	
1951	29.3				−0.04
		0.44	1954	40.6	
1958	32.4				−0.08
1963	37.4	1.00	1958	40.3	0.20
		0.72	1963	41.3	0.02
1968	41.0		1967	41.4	
		0.10			0.43
1970	41.2[a]				
1973	42.2[a]	0.33	1970	42.7	

SOURCES: See text; Mueller and Hamm, 'Trends in industrial market concentration'.
[a] Based on 40 industries only, excluding hosiery and other knitted goods (MLH 417) and bricks, fireclay and refactory goods (MLH 461).

Table 2.9 indicates an increase in average three-enterprise employment concentration of 13 percentage points in the United Kingdom from 29 per cent in 1951 to 42 per cent in 1973. This contrasts with a small rise of only 2 percentage points in United States four-enterprise shipments concentration from 41 per cent in 1947 to 43 per cent in 1970. The different definitions of industry mean that the levels of concentration are not comparable, but the difference in concentration trends is very marked.

[1] Mueller and Hamm, 'Trends in industrial market concentration'.

Prior to 1958, the United States experienced slight falls in concentration, whilst the United Kingdom experienced a rise of about 0.4 percentage points per annum during 1951–8. As shown in this chapter, this follows a concentration increase of about 0.2 percentage points per annum for 1935–51. While the United States experienced small to moderate concentration increases in the 1960s, the United Kingdom experience was markedly different with rises of about 1.0 percentage points per annum in 1958–63 and 0.7 percentage points per annum in 1963–8. Although limitations in the data probably mean that the 1968–70 average concentration ratios are not comparable, there is some evidence of decleration in the concentration increase in 1970–3.

Table 2.10. *Changes in concentration and in employment weights of comparable industries since 1951*

	1951	1958	1958	1968	1970	1973
Mean concentration (%)						
Current weights	23.2	26.8	33.8	44.6	42.0	42.5
Equal weights	31.2	33.9	36.9	45.6	47.4	48.2
Difference	−8.0	−7.1	−3.1	−1.0	−5.4	−5.7
Ratios[a]						
Differences		0.89		0.32		1.06
Mean weights		1.04		0.96		0.96
Covariances		0.92		0.31		1.01

SOURCES: Tables 2.2, 2.3 and 2.6.
[a] 1958/1951, 1968/1958 and 1973/1970.

Table 2.10 summarises changes in the average concentration ratio of comparable sets of industries in the periods 1951–8, 1958–68 and 1970–3. It also decomposes the effects of changes in the employment weights, using equation (2A.8) from appendix 2A. It can also be seen from table 2.10 that in each of the years studied the equally weighted mean was greater than the mean obtained by using current-year employment as weights. This implies that covariance of employment and concentration ratios across industries is negative. This negative covariance did not change much between 1970 and 1973, as is also shown, but its absolute value fell sharply between 1958 and 1968. Thus after 1968 the change in mean concentration was much the same for both means, but for the earlier period 1951–68 the equally weighted mean gave a slightly lower increase in concentration. But this difference is too small to affect our basic conclusion that most of the concentration increase since 1951 must be attributed to the average tendency for all industries to increase their concentration ratios and not to any tendency for the high-concentration industries to grow relative to others. The equally weighted mean is therefore sufficient to measure the growth of industrial concentration.

Is it too soon to say whether the moderation of the rate of concentration increase observed in the period 1970–3 represents another example of an economic trend coming to a premature end? The answer to this question must await the publication of more up-to-date industry concentration ratios in the Censuses of Production, although the product concentration ratios for 1975 used in the next chapter also suggest that the upward trend in concentration has come to a halt. Meanwhile we should do well to heed the words of Cairncross:[1]

> A trend is a trend is a trend
> But the question is, will it bend?
> Will it alter its course
> Through some unforeseen force
> And come to a premature end?
> *Stein Age Forecaster*

Nevertheless, it has been demonstrated in this chapter that industry concentration in the United Kingdom has increased substantially since 1935 in contrast with the United States experience. This evidence alone has important implications for all those concerned with the problems of monopolisation in United Kingdom industry.

---

[1] A. K. Cairncross, 'Economic forecasting', *Economic Journal*, vol. 79, 1969, pp. 747–812.

THE GROWTH OF CONCENTRATION AT PRODUCT LEVEL

INTRODUCTION

In this chapter the average levels and changes in product concentration are reviewed for the period 1958–75. The level of aggregation is lower (that is, the detail is greater) than the industry or MLH level considered in chapter 2; in international statistics the product level roughly corresponds to the four-digit level. The major reason for measuring concentration at the four-digit level is that a census product is usually much closer to the everyday concept of a market. High levels and large increases in product concentration are signs that the product markets concerned are likely to be, or are tending to become, monopolistic and require further investigation. Because products are more narrowly defined than are MLHs the average product concentration ratios are higher than those studied in chapter 2. The tendency for concentration ratios to increase with smaller groupings is important because the share of the largest enterprise in the market is one criterion used to determine whether it should be investigated by the Monopolies Commission. Originally this critical share was a third and now it is a quarter, but since the concept of a market is inevitably somewhat vague, it is possible to make most large enterprises have shares greater than a quarter by defining the market sufficiently narrowly. Because the product level chosen is somewhat arbitrary, and with it the level of concentration, it was decided to pay most attention here to *changes* in absolute levels of concentration.

As mentioned in chapter 2 and shown in chart 1.1, these changes are similar to those at the industry level in 1958–68. This similarity of observed average changes in concentration at the three-digit and four-digit levels of aggregation is reassuring because *a priori* there are several reasons which could be advanced to show why they might differ. The use of sales concentration ratios at the product level introduces the possibility of some double counting, and moreover sales and employment concentration ratios are likely to differ according to the relative capital intensity of the largest firms in an industry.[1] In addition, establishments with less than 25 employees are excluded from the product concentration ratios, while sales

---

[1] Hart, Utton and Walshe *Mergers and Concentration*, pp. 10–12.

of larger establishments, regardless of the MLH in which they are classified, are included. Despite these differences, however, the trends in *average* product and industry concentration ratios of all manufacturing industries are similar.[1]

We follow the pattern of chapter 2 by first measuring the average levels and changes in product concentration for the sub-periods 1958–63 and 1963–8 and for the whole period 1958–68, using samples of comparable products. Slightly different results may be obtained by using different weights to calculate average changes. We compare average changes using equal weights and sales weights. It is argued that the increase in average product concentration from 1958 to 1963 was much the same as that from 1963 to 1968, contrary to the claims that the increase was greater in the latter period made by Elliot,[2] George,[3] Aaronovitch and Sawyer[4] and the government.[5] We then use recently published data to measure the average levels and change in product concentration for the sub-period 1968–75, in which it is shown that there has been a clear deceleration in the upward trend in product concentration. This result is somewhat surprising, but it is consistent with the results obtained in chapter 2 for the period up to 1973.

A classification of product concentration ratios by Industrial Order is provided in appendix 3B. This corresponds to the classification of industrial concentration ratios given in appendix 2D. It reveals the Industrial Orders in which average product concentration is high and increasing, pinpointing those which should be more closely monitored for purposes of competition policy. It also shows that the industrial classification has a significant effect on levels of product concentration but it does not have any significant effect on changes in these levels. Thus there is no need to stratify product concentration ratios by Industrial Order before taking a sample to examine changes in product concentration. The method of sampling used in this chapter is described in appendix 3A, which also contains a detailed description of the sources used.

THE PERIOD 1958–68

1958–63

Concentration ratios are given for 277 products in Summary Table 5 of the

---

[1] Nevertheless it must not be thought that the two types of concentration ratio are always good substitutes for each other. On the contrary, as shown in appendix 3C, the change in the average product concentration ratio in an Industrial Order is generally a poor indicator of the change in the corresponding average industrial concentration ratio, and so the two types of concentration ratio must be analysed separately.

[2] D. Elliott, 'Concentration in UK manufacturing industry', *Trade and Industry*, vol. 16, 1974, pp. 240–1.

[3] George, 'A note on changes in industrial concentration in the United Kingdom'.

[4] Aaronovitch and Sawyer, *Big Business*.

[5] *A Review of Monopolies and Mergers Policy*, Cmnd 7198.

1963 Census of Production. In nine cases they relate to more than five firms and in a further 54 cases ratios are given for 1963 only. This leaves 214 products for which five-firm concentration ratios are available for both years, from which it is possible to measure the change in average product concentration from 1958 to 1963. These products accounted for 50 per cent of sales of principal products by firms employing 25 or more in both years. Table 3.1 gives equally weighted and sales-weighted mean C_5 for these 214

Table 3.1. *Equally weighted and sales-weighted mean* C_5 *for 214 comparable products, 1958 and 1963*

Percentages

	1958	1963	Change in C_5 1958–63		
			In mean	In weights	Total
Equal weights	55.7	58.6	2.9	—	2.9
Sales weights					
1958	54.4	58.4	4.0	0.4	4.4[a]
1963	55.1	58.8	3.7	0.7	4.4[a]

SOURCES: Census of Production 1963, part·131, table 5; Hart, Utton, and Walshe, *Mergers and Concentration*, chapter 3.

[a] At current weights as in table 2.1.

comparable products in 1958 and in 1963. The equally weighted mean concentration ratio increased by 2.9 percentage points from 55.7 per cent in 1958 to 58.6 per cent in 1963. The equally weighted mean of the 268 products in 1963 was 59.6 per cent so that the 54 products without concentration ratios for 1958 included many with above-average concentration ratios. Their exclusion is regrettable, but the Business Statistics Office is unable to provide estimates of concentration for these products in 1958.

The current-year sales-weighted mean concentration ratio of the 214 products increased from 54.4 per cent in 1958 to 58.8 per cent in 1963, or to 58.4 per cent if 1958 sales weights are used, so the increase was of the order of 4 percentage points. The slightly larger rise in the sales-weighted mean indicates a small positive correlation between product sales and increase in concentration.[1] However, this correlation is not large enough to produce different trends in product and industry concentration over the period 1958–63. Finally, the analysis in table 3.1 shows that changes in weights had very little effect on the total change in product concentration

[1] This result differs from that reported in Hart, Utton and Walshe, *Mergers and Concentration* because the sales weights used in its table 3.1, p. 25 were inadvertently the numerators of the sales concentration ratios, whereas the weights used here are the denominators of the sales concentration ratios. The difference in terms of change in concentration is small, of the order of 1 percentage point over the period 1958–63.

in 1958–63. The increase of 4.4 percentage points was largely due to changes in concentration within individual products.

1963–8

A broadly similar pattern of changes in product concentration occurred in the period 1963–8. A comparable sample of 288 products is used to compare mean sales concentration ratios for 1963 and 1968 in table 3.2. The equally weighted mean increased from 61 per cent in 1963 to 65 per cent in 1968. The current-year sales-weighted mean increased slightly more from 63.4 per cent in 1963 to 67.8 per cent in 1968. For this period therefore the discrepancy between the two measures of change was less than in 1958–63. If we include 27 additional non-comparable products in 1968 the equally weighted mean falls from 65.0 per cent to 64.6 per cent and the sales-weighted mean falls from 67.8 per cent to 67.0 per cent; thus the effects of excluding these 27 products are small. The effects of change in sales weights are also small, as can also be seen from table 3.2.

Table 3.2. *Equally weighted and sales-weighted mean C_5 for 288 comparable products, 1963 and 1968*

Percentages

	1963	1968	Change in C_5 1963–8		
			In mean	In weights	Total
Equal weights	61.0	65.0	4.0	—	4.0
Sales weights					
1963	63.4	67.6	4.2	0.2	4.4[a]
1968	63.8	67.8	4.0	0.4	4.4[a]

SOURCES: Census of Production 1968, part 158, table 44; appendix 3A.
[a] At current weights as in table 2.1.

The similarity between the equally weighted and sales-weighted means and mean changes suggests that there was little or no correlation between sales and level of concentration or between sales and changes in concentration, over the period 1963–8. Thus the slight positive correlation between sales and changes in concentration observed for the period 1958–63 was even smaller in the period 1963–8. But a comparison between changes in concentration in the two sub-periods should really be made using the same sample of products, as follows.

1958–68

In order to consider trends in product concentration over the whole ten-year period a sample of 144 comparable products was selected representing 35 per cent of manufacturing and mining sales in 1968. Their mean sales concentration ratios are given in table 3.3. The equally weighted mean

Table 3.3. *Equally weighted and sales-weighted mean C5 for 144 comparable products, 1958, 1963 and 1968*

Percentages

| | 1958 | 1963 | 1968 | Change in C_5 1958–68 | | | 1963–8 minus 1958–63[b] |
				In mean	In weights	Total	
Equal weights	55.4	58.6	63.4	8.0	—	8.0	1.6
Sales weights							
1958	53.3	58.2	63.2	9.9	1.6	11.5[a]	0.1
1963	55.2	59.6	64.7	..	..	..	0.7
1968	56.2	60.2	64.8	8.6	2.9	11.5[a]	0.6

SOURCES: See appendix 3A.
[a] At current weights as in table 2.1.
[b] Standard error is 0.8 in each case.

concentration ratio increased by 8 percentage points in these ten years with a rise of 4.8 points in the five years 1963–8 as compared with a rise of 3.2 points in 1958–63. This slight acceleration of the rate of increase is confirmed using constant sales weights, but not when using current-year sales weights: the total increase in the current-weighted mean C_5 over the period 1958–68 was 11.5 points, as can be seen in table 3.3, and 5.2 points of this occurred in 1963–8 compared with 6.3 points in 1958–63. This discrepancy indicates again that different results are possible using different measures of central tendency, so that it is desirable to use several such measures in considering concentration trends.

The results of table 3.3 are of particular interest, since it has been claimed by some authors that an important acceleration in the rate of concentration increase occurred in the period 1963–8, associated with the known acceleration in merger activity in the second half of the 1960s. George,[1] for example, found that, in a sample of 157 four-digit products, equally weighted average concentration ratios in 1958, 1963 and 1968 were 56.6, 59.6 and 65.4 per cent respectively, leading him to conclude that 'the average increase in concentration for the period 1963–8 was almost twice as high as for the previous five years'. While the magnitude of the concentration increase reported by George for 1963–8 must be treated as suspect because of his failure to exclude products affected by 1967 steel nationalisation from his sample, his general conclusion that the rate of concentration increase accelerated in the late 1960s has been supported by other authors[2] and has been echoed in the government Green Paper,[3] which reports that the rate of concentration increase slowed down in the

[1] George, 'A note on changes in industrial concentration'.
[2] Elliott, 'Concentration in UK manufacturing industry'; Aaronovitch and Sawyer, *Big Business*.
[3] *A Review of Monopolies and Mergers Policy*, Cmnd 7198.

period 1958–63, the main increase in concentration levels occurring between 1963 and 1968.

Table 3.3 shows that there are no grounds for claiming that a sharp acceleration in product concentration occurred in the late 1960s. The difference between the mean increases in the two periods 1958–63 and 1963–8 was only 1.6 percentage points, using equal weights. While this is just significantly different from zero at the 5 per cent level, it is not supported by any of the three weighted means. Each of these shows a much smaller increase, of at most 0.7 percentage points, and none of them is significant on the usual statistical criteria. There is certainly no support for a doubling of the rate of increase. Our conclusion is that the rate of increase in concentration was much the same in the two periods, in spite of the acceleration of merger activity in the second period.

THE PERIOD SINCE 1968

The publication of product concentration ratios for 1975 in *Business Monitor PQ 1006* allows us to measure the trend in average concentration into the 1970s. In particular these data allow us to check the apparent tendency for the rate of concentration increase to decelerate after 1968 as indicated by the average industry concentration ratios of chapter 2. It proved possible to compare 256 selected products over the seven-year period 1968–75, and equally weighted and sales-weighted five-firm product concentration ratios for this period are given in table 3.4.

Table 3.4. *Equally weighted and sales-weighted mean C_5 for 256 comparable products, 1968 and 1975*

Percentages

	1968	1975	Change in C_5 1968–75		
			In mean	In weights	Total
Equal weights	63.4	65.1	1.7	—	1.7
Sales weights					
1968	64.4	65.4	1.0	0.5	1.5[a]
1975	66.1	65.9	−0.2	1.7	1.5[a]

SOURCES: *Business Monitor PQ 1006*; appendix 3A.
[a] At current weights as in table 2.1.

The evidence of table 3.4 suggests on balance that concentration increased only slightly over these seven years. Using equal weights, concentration increased by 1.7 percentage points from 63.4 per cent in 1968 to 65.1 per cent in 1975. This increase is approximately the same as the 1.5 point increase in the current sales-weighted mean from 64.4 to 65.9. Using 1968 sales weights, the concentration increase was lower at 1.0

percentage points, whilst using 1975 sales weights concentration actually fell, albeit marginally. There were 153 products in the sample with concentration increases in the period, compared with 103 with decreases or no change. These findings thus suggest a slight rise in concentration was experienced in the period, a conclusion which conforms with the view of Phillips and Gray of the Business Statistics Office.[1]

The analysis of the change in the current-weighted mean in table 3.4 gives conflicting results. If 1968 weights are used the change in weights was less important than the average increase in concentration within products. If 1975 weights are used the reverse is true: the effect of changes in sales weights easily outweighed the slight decrease in average concentration within products. It is possible that these conflicting results are attributable, at least in part, to changes in the methods of estimating product concentration ratios. Product concentration ratios for 1975 were calculated from the quarterly inquiries into manufacturers' sales conducted by the Business Statistics Office, in contrast with the 1968 ratios which were calculated from the full-scale Census of Production for 1968. These differences in data sources may give rise to comparability biases in the results of table 3.4, although the existence, extent and nature of such biases are difficult for the outside observer to assess. We have already noted in chapter 2 that there are problems associated with the establishment of the new Central Production Register in 1970 which make it difficult to compare concentration ratios for the 1970s with corresponding ratios for 1968. If anything, one would expect *ceteris paribus* some possible upward bias to 1975 concentration arising from the less than full census coverage in that year.

Nevertheless, the consistency of the results in table 3.4 with those presented in table 2.6 above for the limited period 1970–3 is reassuring. Both suggest an important deceleration in the rate of concentration increase in the 1970s compared with the 1960s. Indeed the small concentration increase observed over the seven years covered by table 3.4 suggests that some stabilisation of concentration trends does actually seem to have occurred in United Kingdom manufacturing industry. In so far as this is the case, it can only be welcomed by those who are opposed to the monopolisation of United Kingdom industry.

The conclusions on mean changes in product concentration are based on the various means used in table 3.1, 3.2, 3.3 and 3.4 and the question naturally arises which weighted average should be used. To answer this question we used equation (2A.8) in appendix 2A and repeated the analysis of table 2.10 to compare equally weighted and current sales-weighted mean product concentration ratios, as shown in table 3.5. It can

---

[1] *Trade and Industry*, 17 November 1978, pp. 358–60.

Table 3.5. *Changes in concentration and in sales weights of comparable products since 1958*

	144 products		256 products	
	1958	1968	1968	1975
Mean C_5 (%)				
Current weights	53.3	64.8	64.4	65.9
Equal weights	55.4	63.4	63.4	65.1
Difference	−2.1	1.4	1.0	0.8
Ratios[a]				
Differences		−0.67		0.80
Mean weights		1.65		1.03
Covariances		−1.10		0.82

SOURCES: Tables 3.3 and 3.4; appendix 3A.
[a] 1968/1958 and 1975/1968.

be seen that in the period 1968–75 these two averages give virtually the same results; the ratios are all near unity. We may therefore use the equally weighted mean C_5 on grounds of simplicity. In the period 1958–68 however, the ratios are not near unity so that different results may be obtained by using different means. Whereas in 1958 the level of product concentration was negatively correlated with the level of sales of the product, by 1968 this correlation was positive. Thus the increase of 11.5 percentage points in the current sales-weighted mean between 1958 and 1968 was partly the result of changes in weights: as shown in table 3.3 either 1.6 or 2.9 of these 11.5 points may be attributed to the effects of changes in weights, depending on whether 1958 or 1968 weights are used. Nevertheless, the equally weighted mean increased by 8 percentage points over the same period so most of the concentration increases cannot be attributed to changes in weights. The simple, equally weighted mean C_5 is still a good guide to the direction and amount of change in concentration from 1958 to 1968, but it needs to be supplemented by other types of weighted mean as in tables 3.1 to 3.3.

CONCLUSIONS

The level of a product concentration ratio is a useful indicator of a likely case of oligopoly. The change in this ratio provides even more useful information because the level is affected by the arbitrary definition of a product. These changes were averaged over all products in order to measure general trends. Different mean levels and different mean changes can result from different weighting systems; no single weighting system is correct. The safest procedure is to compute more than one type of average, preferably using at least two means which are thought to reveal the extreme levels and changes within which the remaining weighted means probably occur. Because of the tendency for different weights to produce different results, it is dangerous to compare the different increases in different time periods on the basis of only one type of arithmetic mean. Our conclusion, based on several weighted means, is that the increase in average product concentration from 1958 to 1963 was much the same as that in the period 1963–8, namely of the order of 3 or 4 percentage points. There is certainly no reliable evidence to suggest that there was an acceleration in the increase in product concentration between the first and the second quinquennia within the decade 1958–68.

There is some evidence, however, that there was a strong deceleration in the increase in product concentration within the period 1968–75. Indeed, the 1975 sales-weighted mean level of concentration decreased slightly over these seven years. This surprising 'bend in the trend' may be attributable in part to the change in the methods used by the Business Statistics Office to compile the data, but at least this deceleration is consistent with that observed for industrial concentration for the period since 1968 in chapter 2.

Finally we note the conclusions based on the detailed analysis in appendices 3B and 3C. First, the increase in product concentration was not the same in all Industrial Orders. In 1958–68 six Industrial Orders stand out as including the largest increases in product concentration: Orders XIII (textiles), II (mining and quarrying), III (food, drink and tobacco), XI (vehicles), XV (clothing), and IX (electrical engineering). These sectors had the largest increases in oligopoly in British manufacturing industries, and of these Orders III, IX and XI had high mean levels of product concentration in 1968. In 1968–75 the Industrial Orders with outstanding increases in product concentration were II (mining and quarrying) and XIV (leather and fur). Both were small, with below-average levels of product concentration in 1968, and cannot be regarded as important examples of increasing oligopoly.

Secondly, the Orders with outstanding increases in product concentration from 1958 to 1968 did not, apart from II (mining and quarrying) and possibly XIII (textiles), experience a similar increase in the later period 1968–75. Moreover, some Orders had decreases in average product concentration and this provides a further indication of the dynamic nature of industrial structure. It is quite wrong to suppose that there is an inevitable tendency for concentration to increase continuously in every product group. The lack of such persistence is measured by serial correlation coefficients in chapters 4 and 5.

Thirdly, although in the period 1958–68 the trend in average product and average industrial concentration ratios is much the same, these different types of concentration ratio are not good substitutes for each other in all contexts. The changes in these ratios within any one Industrial Order tend to differ, so that when we are primarily concerned with the broad industrial stratification of concentration changes, it is necessary to analyse industrial and product concentration separately.

4

THE DETERMINANTS OF INDUSTRIAL CONCENTRATION

INTRODUCTION

This chapter provides a statistical analysis of levels and changes in concentration at the MLH (three-digit) level of aggregation; it is at this level rather than at product level that Census of Production data on most of the relevant variables are published. Our first task is to estimate the relative importance of the systematic factors determining the *levels* of industrial concentration. We then attempt to explain *changes* in industrial concentration. In each case we use ordinary least-squares multiple regression analysis so that average relationships are studied. For purposes of economic policy it is useful to know, for example, the average effects of scale-economies in increasing concentration, even though this average effect might not be very relevant if we were investigating changes in concentration in a particular industry. Thus this chapter is concerned with the wood, whereas the next chapter investigates particular trees in it.

Most of the econometric research into the determinants of industrial concentration is American, as are the standard textbooks on the topic. For example, chapter 4 of the textbook by Scherer[1] reviews the following major determinants of market structure: economies of scale, mergers, government policies and, finally, stochastic shocks. A more recent American research paper[2] summarises the various theories of the causes underlying the increases in industrial concentration and adds two more determinants to the list compiled by Scherer: barriers to entry into industries and countervailing power. In this book we confine our attention to the systematic rather than the stochastic forces influencing concentration. This does not mean that we regard the stochastic models as unimportant, but there are good reasons for not introducing them here. To do so would involve major additional research because the appropriate models are far more complicated than those formulated by Scherer and by Ornstein *et al*. The original National Institute study by Hart and Prais[3] modified the simple Gibrat law of proportionate effect by introducing Galtonian

---

[1] F. M. Scherer, *Industrial Market Structure and Economic Performance*, Chicago, Rand McNally, 1971.
[2] S. I. Ornstein, J. F. Weston, M. D. Intriligator and R. E. Shrieves, 'Determinants of market structure', *Southern Economic Journal*, vol. 39, 1973.
[3] Hart and Prais, 'The analysis of business concentration'.

regression and this modification has become even more important in recent years for there is a clear tendency for Galtonian regression away from the median. That is, contrary to Gibrat's law, in recent years in the United Kingdom the proportionate growth of firms has tended to increase with the size of firm. A summary of the evidence is provided by Prais.[1] The Galton model has also been modified by various research workers to include serial correlation. Finally, the stochastic models are most appropriate at the highest levels of aggregation such as the whole of industry, or at least the manufacturing part of it, so that the distribution of individual enterprises may be studied. However, here we are primarily concerned with the stratification of manufacturing into individual industries and products, even though such stratification splits some enterprises and allocates their component parts to different industries. While it would be possible to develop a new and even more complicated stochastic model to incorporate such stratification, this would be unlikely to yield valuable results and would merely distract from the main aim of assessing the importance of the systematic factors affecting concentration. The stochastic forces are important, but in this book their importance is measured by the residuals from regression equations.

The systematic forces investigated in this chapter are economies of scale, industry size, the plant–enterprise ratio, advertising and mergers. The first three variables are used in a multiple regression to 'explain' differences in the levels of concentration *between industries*. To 'explain' changes in industrial concentration over time, the fourth and fifth variables, advertising and expenditure on mergers, are introduced on the right-hand side of a regression, with changes in the other variables and the initial level of concentration. The dependent variable is the proportion of an industry's employment controlled by the five largest enterprises, denoted by C_5. The explanatory variables will be defined in detail later. The year chosen for the analysis of concentration levels is 1968, the most recent year for which comprehensive industry concentration data were available at the time of writing, and the sample consists of 141 manufacturing and mining industries which represent the private sector of industrial production.[2]

ECONOMIES OF SCALE

A primary determinant of enterprise concentration in an industry is the

---

[1] Prais, *Evolution of Giant Firms*.

[2] The Census of Production divided manufacturing and mining into 149 MLHs in 1968. Eight of these industries are dominated by public corporations: coal mining; metalliferous mining and quarrying; coke ovens and manufactured fuel; iron and steel (general); steel tubes; iron castings, etc; locomotives and railway track equipment; and railway carriages, wagons and trams. These eight industries accounted for 11 per cent of employment in all manufacturing and mining industry in 1968.

optimum size of enterprise and the basic technological determinant of this is the optimum size of plant in the industry–namely that at which average costs are minimised. The hypothesis is, therefore, that industries in which technological considerations favour large plants will tend to have higher enterprise concentration than those where small plants are typical, ignoring the possibility of multi-plant enterprises which will be discussed later.

In practice the distribution of plant sizes in an industry tends to be positively skew, with only a few plants in the upper tail. This may be partly explained by the diversity of the products of an industry. While large plants may offer advantages in the production of standardised products with large sales, they are almost by definition not suited to producing specialised products. It is typically in this field therefore that medium-sized and small plants, often using quite different technologies from their larger rivals, are able to hold their own. Thus the size distribution of plants for producing a particular specialised product might well be nearly symmetrical with most plants near the mean or median size of that distribution. The same could easily be true for the comparatively few large plants making a standardised product. But although both size distributions are nearly symmetrical they have widely different means. The result is that, when the component parts of a census industry are combined in order to obtain a size distribution of plants for a complete industry, a positively skew distribution emerges. The attribution of skewness to the aggregation of near symmetrical distributions with different means has been used by Miller[1] to explain the positive skewness of income distributions. In the present context of industrial concentration, it could be argued, for example, that the size distributions of plants making breakfast cereals, or milling flour, are approximately symmetrical, but have different means. The size distribution of plants in grain milling, the census industry to which these two principal products are allocated, together with many others, is positively skew because few of the principal products are like breakfast cereals which have a relatively large optimum size of plant. Unfortunately, the size distribution of plants at the level of a principal product is not published, so the data available do not permit a test of this aggregation hypothesis, but it seems highly plausible.

Nevertheless, it is not a complete explanation of the positively skew size distribution of plants. It is also reasonable to suppose that the size distribution of plants is influenced by some form of stochastic process, similar to the Gibrat or Galton models used to explain the generation of the size distribution of firms, with plants changing their sizes by random proportionate disturbances. If there is no Galtonian regression towards the

[1] H. P. Miller, *Income of the American People*, New York, Wiley, 1955.

median, the skewness of the size distribution of plants would tend to increase over time, even within each specialised section of a census industry.

Given that the only data available are in the form of a size distribution of plants for a whole industry, it is necessary to base a measure of optimal plant scale on these data. The measure chosen is the median of the first-moment distribution of plants by employment used by Florence[1] and by Weiss.[2] We call it the Florence-median. It is the hypothetical plant at the mid-point of the employment array so that half of the employment of an industry comes from plants larger than this and half from smaller plants. This measure is superior to the mean and median of the original distribution, both of which are heavily affected by the number of plants in the industry. On the other hand, the Florence-median does suffer the disadvantage that it must be estimated by interpolation, or in some cases by extrapolation, so that measurement errors may become important, a disadvantage not shared by average plant size.[3]

The use of the Florence-median to measure plant economies of scale is based on the assumption that this parameter of the size distribution is highly correlated with the technical concept of minimum efficient scale of plant. Little is known about this latter concept, but estimates based on hypothetical engineering data are available.[4] Bearing in mind that they exclude the effects of transport costs, which may enable plants in some industries to operate efficiently at sizes well below the technical minimum efficient scale, we regard the correspondence between the Florence-median and the minimum efficient scale as sufficiently close to justify using our measure of plant economies of scale in a regression analysis to determine industrial concentration. Further support for this belief is provided by the correlation between the Florence-median and the estimates of the minimum efficient scale made by Rees,[5] based on the 'survivor' technique, which is thought by many economists to yield reasonably good estimates of the optimum size of plant.[6]

[1] P. S. Florence, *The Logic of Industrial Organisation*, London, Kegan Paul, Trench, Trubner, 1933.
[2] L. W. Weiss, 'Factors in changing concentration', *Review of Economics and Statistics*, vol. 45, 1963, pp 70–7.
[3] The majority of estimates required interpolation, which was done linearly, and involved relatively small margins of error. In the few cases where extrapolation was required, linear estimates in many cases proved nonsensical, and extrapolation was instead carried out on log-probability paper. In these cases, the margin for error was often very large.
[4] *A Review of Monopolies and Mergers Policy*, Cmnd 7198, pp. 87–8. The estimates listed there are compared where possible with estimates of the Florence-median in appendix 4A.
[5] R. D. Rees, 'Optimum plant size in United Kingdom industries: some survivor estimates', *Economica*, vol. 40 (new series), 1973.
[6] This does not imply that we accept the 'survivor' technique estimate. On the contrary, if the size distribution of plants is influenced by a Gibrat or Galton stochastic process, with plants moving through size classes over time, any method of estimating the minimum efficient scale based on univariate size distributions is obviously suspect. Bivariate size distributions of the *same* plants at the

SIZE OF INDUSTRY MEASURED BY EMPLOYMENT

The inclusion of industry size as a variable is easily explained. We have suggested that the size of a firm is primarily determined by the optimum plant size of an industry. It follows that the share of the leading firms in total industry output (the concentration ratio) depends on optimum plant size relative to industry size; and we expect a negative partial correlation between the concentration ratio and industry size when the latter accompanies the Florence-median plant size on the right-hand side of a multiple regression equation. We already know from chapter 2 that the simple negative correlation between industry size (measured by employment) and concentration in 1968 was small, because the 1968 employment-weighted and equally weighted means were similar. In fact the simple correlation coefficients in 1968 between employment concentration and the alternative measures of industry size were 0.0634 (using gross output), −0.0632 (using net output) and −0.1654 (using employment), with $n = 141$ in each case. The output correlations are not significant. If the logarithm of employment is used, $r = -0.23$, which is significant, but the use of logarithms does not improve the performance of the output variables.

We used three measures of industry size in our regressions: gross output (goods produced and work done), net output and total employment.[1] The variables were used independently and as the denominator of a variable with the Florence-median plant size as the numerator. Better results were obtained using them independently; in addition employment proved the best measure.[2] The results reported below are therefore those in which size is represented by employment.

THE PLANT–ENTERPRISE RATIO

So far we have ignored the possibility of multi-plant operation by enterprises. On average, taking all enterprises in all industries, the ratio of plants to enterprises was only 1.38 (0.04).[3] However, this figure reflects the fact that small firms typically operate a single plant; large enterprises, on the other hand, are typically multi-plant. In 1968 the average ratio of

two dates are required to measure any tendency for plants of a particular size to 'survive': the existing measurements based on univariate size distributions may identify the size class with an increased market share, but if few plants stay in that class for very long it cannot be regarded as measuring an optimum size in any economic sense.
[1] These data are derived from Summary Table 1 of the 1968 Census.
[2] Best because of highest $\bar{R}^2$s; this superiority might arise because employment is the denominator of the dependent variable.
[3] These figures refer to a sample of 76 industries in 1968 which is used later in the section on changes in concentration. Standard errors of the means are given in brackets.

plants to enterprises for the five largest enterprises was 10.20 (1.32). It is therefore necessary to relax the assumption that all firms operate a single plant and modify our regression equations accordingly.

The view taken here is that the economies of multi-plant operation differ between industries, and that a reasonable proxy for the combined relative importance of these economies is the ratio of all plants to all enterprises in the industry. We assume that a positive partial correlation between this ratio and the concentration ratio indicates that the availability of multi-plant economies implies higher concentration.

REGRESSION RESULTS USING LEVELS OF CONCENTRATION

The discussion in the previous sections of this chapter suggests that the level of industrial concentration may be explained by plant economies of scale (as measured by the Florence-median), by the size of industry and by the economies of multi-plant operation (as measured by the ratio of plants to enterprises in each industry). Since there is no rigorous mathematical economic theory available from which to derive the precise form of the relationship between these explanatory variables and the level of concentration, we have to rely on empirical tests to reveal the most appropriate regression specification. A convenient starting-point is to specify a linear relationship between the variables and this yields the results in the first column of table 4.1.

Table 4.1. *Determinants of the differences in levels of concentration, C_5, between 141 manufacturing industries, 1968[a]*

	Equation		
	Linear	Log-linear	Semi-log
Constant	21.55	2.09	−19.37
	(4.76)	(0.13)	(4.45)
Economies of scale	0.009	0.38	15.81
	(0.001)	(0.02)	(0.71)
Industry size	−0.08	−0.24	−10.28
	(0.02)	(0.02)	(0.80)
Plant–enterprise ratio	16.43	0.56	27.78
	(3.26)	(0.10)	(3.54)
$\bar{R}^2$	0.472	0.783	0.852

SOURCES: See text.
[a] Standard errors in brackets.

The first result is encouraging. Each regression coefficient is significantly different from zero, each has the sign expected from the discussion in the previous sections and the overall goodness of fit, as measured by

$\bar{R}^2 = 0.472$, is quite high and indicates that the variables on the right-hand side explain nearly half of the variation of concentration ratios between industries.

A log-linear regression is summarised in the second column. It can be seen that each of the regression coefficients is significantly different from zero, that the overall goodness of fit is even higher than in the first column, and that the standard errors of each coefficient are lower. Indeed the results of the log-linear regression are so much better than those of the linear model that the question arises whether the results are too good, merely being produced by a near-identity. The problem of near-identities in estimated regression relationships in this field has concerned research workers for many years. We discuss the problem in appendix 4B, but it is worth stressing at this stage that the Florence-median is not the arithmetic mean size of plant but the median of the first-moment distribution of plants by employment. In addition, we use an alternative semi-logarithmic specification in the third column of table 4.1, in which this problem does not arise, except perhaps as an approximation. The results in this column are even better than those in the second and confirm that the important determinants of the inter-industry level of industrial concentration are plant economies of scale, industry size and the plant–enterprise ratio.

In interpreting this semi-logarithmic regression we assume that the variables on the right-hand side are fixed by repeated sampling. This is hardly realistic in the present context. When comparing the distributions of these variables across industries, it seems preferable to regard each as a sample marginal distribution drawn from some population with a multivariate distribution. The form of this distribution will determine the form of the regression. There are good reasons for assuming that the relevant distribution is multivariate and log-normal. The marginal distributions in this case would be univariate log-normal and would be consistent with the result noted by Aitchison and Brown[1] that an industrial classification of an economic variable often produces a log-normal distribution. They also provide a theory of breakage or classification to explain this phenomenon. If we assume multivariate log-normality, the appropriate regression is that in the second column of table 4.1. Moreover, it has all the convenient statistical properties needed to obtain good estimates.

It can be seen that the largest elasticity is that on the plant–enterprise ratio, with economies of scale having the second largest effect. This of course assumes that the concentration ratio is the dependent variable. But it could be argued that an increase in this ratio, as the result of mergers for example, would tend to increase the ratio of plants to enterprises. It might

---

[1] J. Aitchison and J. A. C. Brown, *The Lognormal Distribution*, Cambridge University Press, 1957.

also increase the Florence-median size of plant if small plants were closed down in some 'rationalization' process and workers were transferred to larger plants or made redundant. In order to allow for the effects of mergers, we include expenditure on mergers as an explanatory variable in the next section on *changes* in concentration.

REGRESSION RESULTS USING PROPORTIONATE CHANGES IN CONCENTRATION

If the Florence-median plant size, the industry size and the plant–enterprise ratio explain the level of concentration in an industry, changes in these variables should play some part in the explanation of changes in industrial concentration. It is possible that the period for which such changes are measured is too short to allow much variation between industries, and this is particularly relevant for changes in plant economies of scale. The most we can do to reveal such changes is to maximise the time interval studied and, from the data which were available at the time of writing, this maximum is the decade 1958–68. It is also possible that additional variables become important when changes in concentration are being investigated. For example, we should expect that the extent of merger activity over the decade would explain part of the increase in concentration.

A purely statistical reason for expecting some differences between the equations explaining levels and those explaining changes in concentration is that the samples of industries chosen tend to differ. In each case the largest samples available are selected, but as a result of changes in the S I C over time, the sample of comparable industries used to measure changes tends to be smaller than that used to measure levels. In the present case, the sample of comparable industries is 76 (that is the 79 comparable over 1958–68 from chapter 2 minus three classified in mining) compared with the 141 industries used for the level of concentration in the previous section. There is no reason to suppose that the 76 comparable industries are representative of the 141 industries in 1968; the 65 non-comparable industries tend to be those with important changes in composition, due to the growth of new products or to the decline of old products, and they may well differ in their concentration characteristics from the more stable comparable industries.

Changes in variables may be measured absolutely or proportionately. Absolute changes, or first differences, would lead to a model corresponding to the linear regression equation in table 4.1 which was rejected in the previous section. The first differences between the logarithms of all variables would correspond to the logarithmic regression in table 4.1, which was considered attractive from a theoretical point of view and which

Table 4.2. *Determinants of the variation in the changes in concentration between 76 comparable industries, 1958–68[a]*

	Equation number			
	(1)	(2)	(3)	(4)
Constant	0.18	0.86	0.75	0.75
	(0.05)	(0.14)	(0.14)	(0.14)
Economies of scale	0.32	0.29	0.30	0.29
	(0.14)	(0.12)	(0.11)	(0.11)
Industry size	−0.36	−0.31	−0.28	−0.29
	(0.13)	(0.11)	(0.11)	(0.11)
Plant–enterprise ratio	0.35	0.59	0.51	0.53
	(0.35)	(0.31)	(0.29)	(0.30)
Initial concentration		−0.20	−0.24	−0.24
		(0.04)	(0.04)	(0.04)
Mergers			0.08	0.08
			(0.03)	(0.03)
Advertising				0.02
				(0.03)
$\bar{R}^2$	0.13	0.34	0.40	0.40

SOURCES: See text and appendix 4C.
[a] Standard errors in brackets.

provided a good fit. The first difference between the logarithms of concentration ratios in each industry in 1958 and 1968 is the dependent variable in table 4.2, namely log C_5 (1968) − log C_5 (1958). The first three explanatory variables are logarithmic changes in the measures of plant economies of scale, industry size, and the ratio of plants to enterprises. The regression results are summarised in the first column of table 4.2. While each coefficient has the expected sign, only those on economies of scale and industry size are significantly different from zero. Moreover $\bar{R}^2$ is very low. To improve the specification it is necessary to include more of the large number of factors which affect the logarithmic changes in concentration. Some of these factors are measurable but others are not, so that we must not expect to explain all of the concentration change. Three plausible additional variables are proposed here: the initial concentration level, advertising and mergers.

The initial concentration level

Various reasons may be adduced for suspecting that there will be an inverse relationship between concentration change and the initial level of concentration (log C_5). It is possible that the most important is purely statistical: the restriction that the concentration ratio must take a value between zero and 100 per cent makes for a negative correlation between concentration change and the initial concentration level. Whilst an industry with an initial concentration level of 50 per cent may experience a possible concentration rise or fall of 50 points, an industry with an initial level of 90 per cent can have a maximum concentration rise of only 10 points and one with an initial level of 10 per cent a maximum fall of only 10 points. This ceiling and floor to the change in the concentration ratio of industries with either very high or very low concentration ratios thus produces a negative correlation between change and level of concentration. Another way of summarising the statistical effect of the initial concentration level on the change in concentration is to use the Galtonian model of regression towards the mean. Since $\Delta \log C = \log C_5 \ (1968) - \log C_5 \ (1958)$, we may take $-\log C_5 \ (1958)$ to the right-hand side of the equation in the second column of table 4.2 to obtain the partial regression coefficient of $\log C_5 \ (1968)$ on $\log C_5 \ (1958)$ namely $1 - 0.20 = 0.80$. Because 0.80 is less than one, Galtonian regression towards the mean occurred over the period 1958–68.

But such regression may not be purely statistical: there may be economic forces at work which tend to pull industries with extremely high or low levels of concentration towards more central levels. For example, suppose the five top enterprises have 90 per cent of the output of an industry. If they use their market power to raise prices or lower quality they might well lose business to the smaller firms already in the industry. If they simply rest on their laurels they could also lose trade to the small firms. In both cases the concentration ratio would fall; the oligopolists sow the seeds of their own destruction by acting as if they need not bother with outside competition. These hypothetical economic examples might explain why there is an *average tendency* for industries with extremely high concentration ratios to regress towards the mean level of concentration. Of course this is quite consistent with the observation that *some* industries have persistently high levels of concentration as the result of entry barriers such as extensive advertising.

Advertising

A second hypothesis is that the proportionate change in concentration is positively related to the level of advertising expenditure. The relationship between market structure and advertising is complex and limitations on data preclude a detailed examination. Instead, let us consider the simple hypothesis that the ratio of advertising to sales in 1968 had a positive effect on the change in concentration between 1958 and 1968. Tacitly this assumes that the 1968 advertising–sales ratio gives a good guide to relative advertising rates throughout the 1960s. Given this, we might expect high advertising levels to permit leading firms in highly concentrated industries to maintain or increase their market share, while at the same time exercising some degree of market power. This variable might thus be regarded as countering some of the effects of initial high levels of concentration which tend to reduce concentration. The advertising data in the Census of Production suffer from the defect that individual observations are not available on all 76 industries. In the 42 cases where data are available in group form only, the advertising–sales ratio for the group was applied to the individual industries.

Mergers

Finally, we should expect merger-intensive industries to experience greater increases in concentration. It could be argued that mergers are but a means towards increased concentration rather than in some sense a fundamental cause of it. On the other hand, there may well be an effect independent of the other variables on the right-hand side of our equations which justifies its inclusion. Unfortunately data on mergers are not available at the MLH level, so that it was necessary to use data at the Industrial Order (two-digit) level, allocating the same value to each MLH in an Order. The variable used was expenditure on mergers 1958–68 divided by 1958 net assets, and this relates only to a sample of enterprises in each Order. Clearly, the variable is somewhat crude and does not capture the total effect of mergers in increasing concentration. All the change variables were measured as the 1968 value divided by the 1958 value, so that no change is given as unity.

Table 4.2 presents the results of adding these three variables. Each variable has the expected sign, although the ratio of plants to enterprises, and the advertising–sales ratio have no significant effect. The introduction of the initial concentration level in the second column dramatically increases the value of $\bar{R}^2$. However, the parameters associated with the other significant variables are only slightly affected by this addition, giving support to the specification. Similarly, the introduction of merger expenditure, log M, in the third and fourth columns has little effect on the parameters and increases $\bar{R}^2$ to 0.40.

The failure of the advertising–sales ratio, log A/S, to affect the change in enterprise concentration is an important result.[1] While it has already been noted that there were specification and measurement problems associated with this variable, a permanent feature of the various regressions attempted, besides those reported in table 4.2, was the complete non-significance of this variable. Thus it appears, contrary to much *a priori*

---

[1] This is consistent with the findings for the United States in S. I. Ornstein and S. Lustgarten, 'Advertising intensity and industrial concentration – an empirical inquiry 1947–1967' in D. G. Tuerck (ed.), *Issues in Advertising*, Washington (D.C.), American Enterprise Institute for Public Policy Research, 1978; but not with those of Mueller and Hamm, 'Trends in industrial market concentration'.

speculation, that the advertising–sales ratio in an industry has no effect on changes in concentration.

Mueller and Hamm, in their study of trends in market concentration for the United States, found an important distinction between such trends in producer- and consumer-goods industries. In a sample of 166 four-digit industries there was a moderate increase in concentration among consumer-goods industries over the period 1947 to 1970, but a small decrease in concentration among producer-goods industries. Moreover, when dummy variables were introduced to reflect high and moderate product differentiation in consumer-goods industries relative to producer-goods industries, they had a strong and significantly positive effect on concentration. These effects cannot, however, be detected in United Kingdom data over the period 1958–68. For example, when the residuals of equation (3) in table 4.2 are regressed on $\log A/S$ with dummy variables for intercept and slope ($D = 1$ for producer goods and $D = 0$ for consumer goods) the following results were obtained (with standard errors in brackets).

$$\text{Residuals} = \underset{(0.046)}{0.044} \underset{(0.068)}{-0.103} D + \underset{(0.046)}{0.004} \log A/S$$

$$\underset{(0.073)}{-\ 0.037}\ (\log A/S)\ D \qquad \bar{R}^2 = 0.0365$$

It can be seen that the intercept dummy variable reveals some tendency for producer-goods industries to have smaller concentration increases on average, but the difference is not significant at the 5 per cent level. Advertising has no significant effect on the residuals for consumer-goods or for producer-goods industries. This, and many other tests performed, reveal no reason for believing that advertising has a differential effect on concentration change between consumer-goods and producer-goods industries in the United Kingdom.

In contrast, the mergers variable was significant in our regression despite the fact that its measurement was perhaps even cruder than that of the advertising–sales ratio. The positive coefficient on this variable shows that industries in Orders with relatively high expenditure on mergers during the period had faster increases in concentration. This finding confirms expectations and there seems little room for doubt that an even stronger relationship would have been found if merger data had been available at the MLH level. We provide a more technical discussion of the effects of mergers on concentration in appendix 4B, where we argue that these effects were very important in the period 1958 to 1968.

However, as indicated in table 4.2, many other factors were also at work, a very large number of which produced concentration changes over time. For example, whereas concentration levels are closely associated with plant scale-economies, the results in table 4.2 indicate that logarithmic change in this variable is merely one of many forces at work producing concentration change. That is, these results lend no support to those who contend that the increase in enterprise concentration over time results primarily from the technological need for larger plants. This factor explains only a small part of the change in concentration, while the argument that firm economies of scale (as measured by plant–enterprise ratios) promote concentration increase receives no support at all. Thus, these results are inconsistent with the view that increased industrial concentration is a technological inevitability. Indeed, whether such increases are inevitable at all is a question which may be considered in the context of the persistence of increases in concentration.

If increases in industrial concentration were inevitable, because for example economies of scale ensure that large firms drive out small firms, there would be a strong tendency for increases in concentration in most industries to persist through time; an increase in concentration in an industry in one period would generate a further increase in the following period. This tendency would be measured by a positive correlation across industries between changes in concentration in consecutive periods. On the other hand, if increases in concentration were entirely the result of windfall gains, followed by windfall losses in the next period, there would be a negative correlation between concentration changes across industries.

It is convenient to estimate this association between concentration changes by regressing the change in the period 1963–8 on the change in 1958–63 for the 76 comparable industries in table 4.2. This regression was -0.103 (± 0.094). Although this coefficient has a negative sign, it is not significantly different from zero. There is no support whatsoever for the belief that increases in concentration are technologically inevitable even though *on average* industrial concentration increases over time. The negative sign lends a little support to the windfall gains and losses hypothesis, but the economic forces tending to counteract increases or decreases in concentration were not strong enough to produce a significantly negative regression coefficient.

CONCLUSIONS

The regression analysis used to estimate the determinants of the variation of *levels* of concentration between industries showed that plant economies of scale (measured by the Florence-median), industry size and the plant–enterprise ratio were the most important explanatory variables. Of course this is an average result: many other variables would feature in the explanation of the concentration ratio for one particular industry, and superimposed on all these significant systematic forces would be a multitude of small forces which collectively are commonly called 'chance' or 'stochastic' factors.

When considering changes in the degree of concentration, these stochastic factors become rather more important. Changes in plant economies of scale still have a significant effect, but over a decade such as 1958–68 large changes in this explanatory variable cannot be expected. Changes in the plant–enterprise ratio are even less important and have no significant effect. However, changes in industry size, measured by the numbers employed, are significant. Even so, these systematic variables explained very little of the changes in concentration.

Consequently three additional explanatory variables were added in an attempt to improve the explanation of changes in concentration: initial concentration level, advertising and mergers. The initial concentration level had a clear effect showing that the more highly concentrated industries tend to have lower increases in concentration than the rest. As shown in appendix 4B, the logarithm of concentration in 1958 explained about 22 per cent of the variation in the dependent variable, while the addition of the three systematic variables just discussed added a further 17 per cent. Also interesting is the effect of introducing mergers between 1958 and 1968 to explain the increase in concentration. Due to the limitations of the data, the measurement of mergers is far from ideal. Nevertheless, mergers had a significant positive effect and increased the explained variation by another 4.6 per cent as shown by the analysis of variance in appendix 4B. This success was not repeated for advertising, which was found to have no significant effect on changes in concentration.

Thus, less than half the change in business concentration at industry level can be attributed to increases in plant size, to decreases in industry size and to mergers. Moreover, these factors were not powerful enough to produce a tendency for increases in concentration to persist from 1958–63 to 1963–8. Thus it cannot be argued that systematic and pervasive factors produce inevitable increases in concentration in United Kingdom manufacturing industries. Systematic factors play a role in changing concentration, but it seems likely that a great number of other factors not specified in our regression equations are also important. Some of these factors will have small or industry-specific effects and are perhaps best consigned to the disturbance term in regression analysis. Other factors may have larger effects but are difficult to measure and so have not been considered in this chapter. Such factors are best considered in a case-by-case approach, to which we now turn in order to supplement our understanding of the reasons for changes in concentration.

5

THE DETERMINANTS OF CHANGES IN PRODUCT
CONCENTRATION

INTRODUCTION

Some of the factors tending to change product concentration are investigated in this chapter. The selection of these factors is constrained by the very limited census data at the product level. The regression analyses used in chapter 4 to estimate the importance of the various forces influencing changes in concentration at the industry level cannot be repeated here because data on the important 'explanatory' variables are not available at the product level. Consequently, a descriptive rather than a statistical approach is adopted, based on case studies of a random sample of 30 products published in an interim report in 1973.[1] The results in the present chapter, when compared with the equations in chapter 4, identify the main systematic factors changing concentration and provide an assessment of their relative importance.

Concentration ratios for 1968 were not available when the interim report was being prepared and the most that could be done was to study the changes in concentration ratios of the comparable 214 products over the period 1958–63. Since it was impracticable to undertake a case study for each of these 214 product markets, it was decided to select a random sample of 30 products. One object was to assess the importance of mergers compared with the differential internal growth of enterprises in the increase in product concentration. The case studies in the interim report included information on mergers after 1963, but because data on concentration for 1968 were not available, the contribution of mergers to increases in concentration in the period 1963–8 could not be assessed. This gap is now filled. In addition, it is possible to note the differences between changes in concentration and the role of mergers in the two sub-periods 1958–63 and 1963–8. In particular, it is possible to measure whether the direction and amount of change in concentration in the first sub-period persisted in the second. This persistence of the change in concentration may also be measured for the periods 1963–8 and 1968–75, as a result of the recent publication of data for 1975.

The average change in concentration and the average effects of mergers

[1] Hart, Utton and Walshe, *Mergers and Concentration.*

and of product growth are discussed in the next section. The following sections deal in more detail with increases and decreases in concentration. There are frequent references to the case studies, but no summaries are provided. The technical details of samples can be found in appendix 5A.

THE ROLE OF MERGERS IN CHANGING PRODUCT CONCENTRATION
1958–68

For technical reasons explained in appendix 5A, it was necessary to eliminate three products from the random sample of 30 in order to obtain useful estimates of product concentration for 1968. Table 5.1 gives the equally weighted mean concentration ratio and the current sales-weighted mean concentration ratio for the residual sample of 27 and for the 144 comparable products considered in chapter 3. It can be seen that the levels in the sample of 27 are slightly below those for all 144 comparable products, but the changes are similar for both sets of data.

Table 5.1. *Mean product concentration ratios, 1958, 1963 and 1968*

Percentages

	1958	1963	1968	Change 1958–63	Change 1963–8
Random sample of 27					
Equally weighted	53.4	57.0[a]	62.0	+3.6	+4.8
Sales-weighted	52.6	58.8[a]	63.8	+6.2	+4.9
Comparable products (144)					
Equally weighted	55.4	58.6	63.4	+3.2	+4.8
Sales-weighted	53.3	59.6	64.8	+6.3	+5.2

SOURCES: Hart, Utton and Walshe, *Mergers and Concentration*; table 3.3.
[a] Revised in the 1968 Census; the exactly comparable figures with 1968 were 57.2 and 58.9.

The fact that the changes in the equally weighted mean for the sample of 27 and for all comparable products are similar, supports our decision to assess the effects of mergers in increasing concentration by using the small sample. The major advantage from so doing is that it is possible to use the case studies for each of the sampled products in order to estimate whether mergers were the major cause of an increase in concentration. Such case studies are highly labour-intensive because they involve widespread perusal of trade journals, and extensive correspondence and discussions with many experts in the relevant government departments, trade associations and, above all, in the firms involved in making the products. While the use of a small sample makes it possible to compile case studies, this has to be paid for by a reduction in accuracy which is formally reflected in increases in the standard errors of the estimated changes.

This reduction in accuracy must be borne in mind when inspecting table 5.2, which classifies the sample products by direction of change in concentration, with and without mergers, and by direction of change in output. The major differences between table 5.2 and its counterpart table 3.7 in the interim report[1] are the reduction by three of the number of products (that is 10 per cent of the original number) and the doubling of the time period to the whole decade 1958 to 1968.

Table 5.2. *Classification of a random sample of 27 products by concentration change, change in output and merger activity, 1958–68*

Change in concentration	Change in output			
	Expanding		Stationary or declining	
Increase with mergers	Flour confectionery Contractors' plant Electric cables, etc. Telephone installations Line apparatus Trailers and caravans Other garments (knitted outerwear) Corsets and brassieres Builders' woodwork		Mining machinery Flax Wool sorting, etc. Jute, yarn and cloth Woven carpets	
Number	14	9		5
Increase without mergers	Organic chemicals Washing machines Asbestos manufactures Heavy overalls		Narrow fabrics (non-elastic) Hats	
Number	6	4		2
Decrease	Whisky Detergents Synthetic carpets Fellmongery Wallpaper		Pulp-making machinery, etc. Boilers and boilerhouse plant	
Number	7	5		2
Total	27	18		9

SOURCES: See appendix 5A

Table 5.2 suggests that in about a quarter of the products concentration fell, whereas table 3.7 in the interim report suggested about a third decreased their concentration ratios between 1958 and 1963. Table 5.2 is consistent with the fall in concentration in about a quarter of all the 144

[1] Hart, Utton and Walshe, *Mergers and Concentration.*

comparable products over the decade 1958–68 described in appendix 3A.[1]

Of the twenty products with concentration increases, fourteen or over half the 27 products in the sample had concentration increases primarily as the result of mergers. This result is consistent with most of the other work on this period suggesting that mergers had a substantial effect in changing the market structure of products in United Kingdom manufacturing industry.

Each point estimate of a proportion in table 5.2 has a standard error attached to it. For example, the $14/27 = 52$ per cent of products with increases in concentration due to mergers has a standard error of $[(14/27)(13/27)(1/27)]^{\frac{1}{2}} = 9.6$ per cent so the true proportion for all 144 products cannot be estimated with precision. Another important qualification of table 5.2 is that it classifies by attributes, not by amounts. The justification for this, in addition to its giving a useful first impression of the importance of mergers, is that the basic data and, therefore, the amount of concentration change are subject to errors of measurement, whereas the direction of change in concentration and output and the classification with or without mergers are more reliable. But the amounts of change are interesting even if they are subject to error. In the mergers group, average concentration increased by 15.4 percentage points over the whole decade 1958–68 compared with the average increase of 7.8 percentage points in the group without mergers. That is, in this decade mergers tended to bring faster increases in concentration than did differences in internal growth rates of firms.

A comparison of table 5.2 with table 3.7 in the interim report reveals that mergers were of greater importance in increasing concentration over the decade 1958–68 than over the five-year period 1958–63. The principal reason for the difference between these two tables is the entry of five products into the mergers category, because of the importance of mergers in the second sub-period 1963–8, and the departure of only one product (wallpaper) to the decreased concentration category. Two products (contractors' plant and builders' woodwork) had their small falls in concentration in 1958–63 reversed, predominantly due to merger activity, in the period 1963–8. Three other products (mining machinery, woven carpets, and corsets and brassieres) had small non-merger increases in concentration in 1958–63, outweighed by much larger concentration increases – predominantly by merger – in 1963–8.[2] Only asbestos had a

---

[1] For the 27-product sample about one quarter of the products had concentration falls in each of the sub-periods 1958–63 and 1963–8 also. The discrepancy for the 1958–63 sub-period with the findings of Hart, Utton and Walshe reflects the imprecision of point estimates of the population proportion in small samples.

[2] It is interesting to note that Courtaulds took an active part in this merger activity in the case of corsets and brassieres, while mergers in woven carpets were partly prompted by the threat of entry by Courtaulds and Imperial Chemical Industries.

concentration increase predominantly due to mergers in the years 1958–63 and a concentration increase predominantly due to differential internal growth in 1958–68 as a whole. Thus it appears that mergers caused concentration to increase in more products in 1963–8 than in 1958–63. This is consistent with the known acceleration of merger activity in the whole sector of manufacturing and distribution in the second sub-period 1963–8.

Of course any estimate of the contribution of mergers to the average increase in product concentration must depend on the assumptions made about the average change in concentration which would have taken place in the absence of mergers. For example, if we assumed first that, in the absence of mergers, the fourteen products in the first block of table 5.2 would have been distributed between the second and third blocks in the ratio 6:7, with corresponding average changes in concentration, there would have been an average increase of only 0.85 percentage points over the decade 1958–68.[1] Since the actual average increase was 8.4 points, we might argue that mergers were responsible for 89 per cent of the increase over the period, since $(8.4-0.85)/8.4 = 0.89$. But it seems more reasonable to assume, in the light of the analysis of variance results in chapter 4, that concentration would have increased in most of these fourteen products in any case due to factors other than mergers. If we allocate all fourteen to the second block in table 5.2, the average increase in product concentration would have been 4.5 percentage points. This would yield the result that mergers were responsible for 46 per cent of the increase in product concentration.

Thus the estimates of the effects of mergers depend on the kind of assumptions made. From many points of view, the second set of assumptions seems to be more reasonable. We have already seen in chapter 3 that average product concentration hardly changed between 1968 and 1975 in spite of the intensive merger activity recorded in chapter 2 (table 2.8) for the period after 1968. Even if many of these mergers may be classified as vertical or conglomerate at the product (four-digit) level, it is difficult to reconcile any claim that mergers were responsible for 89 per cent of the change in concentration in the decade 1958–68 with the results for the period after 1968, because the implied decrease in the effect of mergers relative to other factors is too great to be plausible. Thus we prefer the second set of assumptions with the implied merger effect of 46 per cent, or roughly one half.

Obviously this estimate of a half is very much an approximation, and has a large standard error which can be reduced only by undertaking

---

[1] The actual decomposition of the mean change is given by:

$$(27) \ (8.4) = (14) \ (15.4) + (6) \ (7.8) - (7) \ (5.1).$$

many more case studies. However, it is consistent with the results of most of the other investigations into the effects of mergers on concentration in this period.[1]

Table 5.2 also classifies products according to growth or decline. Data on real output growth are not always available at product level so that the classification is not exact.[2] No measure of the extent of expansion or contraction is given because of insufficient data on price and physical changes in output. Nevertheless, the classification facilitates a crude test of the null hypothesis that concentration change is independent of output change. A glance at table 5.2 shows that there is no general inverse relationship between the two, because thirteen of the twenty products where concentration increased were expanding. If factors reducing concentration were at work amongst these products, they were outweighed by more powerful factors increasing concentration.[3] On the other hand, there does appear to be an association between products with declining concentration and expanding markets, which is investigated further below.

It is possible that other categorical variables have significant effects on concentration. One interesting hypothesis suggested by American research is that the classification into consumer-goods or producer-goods industries would yield significant results. As already noted in chapter 4, Mueller and Hamm found that a calm surface of practically static average concentration ratios for all industries in the period 1947–70 masked 'substantial undercurrents of change'.[4] In particular, producer-goods industries experienced an equally weighted average concentration fall of 1.3 percentage points. Further division of consumer-goods industries into those with high, moderate and low product differentiation revealed concentration increases of 12.7, 6.4 and 0.4 percentage points respectively. This led them to the hypothesis that advertising was the major force which had increased concentration at the four-digit or product level in the postwar American economy. In particular, the emergence of network television had been an important factor increasing concentration in industries whose characteristics favoured such advertising. However, the present *small* sample of products in table 5.3 reveals no reason to reject the null hypothesis that the direction of concentration change is independent of the

[1] These investigations are summarised in the *Review of Monopolies and Mergers Policy*, Cmnd 7198, p. 99. Our results are inconsistent with those of L. Hannah and J. A. Kay (*Concentration in Modern Industry: Theory, Measurement and the UK Experience*, London, Macmillan, 1977), who assert that mergers were responsible for 116 per cent of the increase in concentration, but their results are seriously biased, as shown in P. E. Hart, 'On bias and concentration', *Journal of Industrial Economics*, vol. 27, 1979.
[2] For the whole decade 1958–68 wallpaper is designated an expanding product. For this longer period nine products, or roughly a third of the representative sample, were contracting or stationary. Again this is not a very encouraging sign for British industry.
[3] That this may in fact be the case at industry level is suggested by the multiple regression in chapter 4.
[4] Mueller and Hamm, 'Trends in industrial market concentration'.

consumer–producer goods dichotomy.[1] Two thirds of the consumer goods in our sample increased their concentration ratios compared with four fifths of the producer goods, but the absolute numbers involved are too small to permit us to be confident that there is a corresponding difference between all consumer goods and all producer goods. Instead we rely on the multiple regressions of chapter 4, using a much larger sample of 76, which showed that advertising does not seem to be related to increases in concentration, even when allowance is made for the consumer–producer goods dichotomy.

Table 5.3. *Classification of a random sample of 27 products by concentration change 1958–68, and by type of product*

	Concentration change 1958–68		
	Rise	Fall	Total
Consumer goods	8	4	12
Producer goods	12	3	15
Total	20	7	27

SOURCES: As table 5.2.

Another interesting classification of the change in product concentration is by the corresponding change in the previous period. It might be argued that products with increases in concentration should be investigated for possible increases in oligopolistic practices and such products are discussed in the next section. But if this increase in concentration in one period is promptly reversed in the following period, there is obviously less need for concern, for any scope for increased oligopolistic practices has clearly been not so great as to ensure a permanent rise in concentration. Indeed it is possible that the change in the concentration ratio for any product in any one year is abnormal and merely the result of windfall gains in market shares. Thus before investigating any particular product for possible oligopolistic practices, it is advisable to establish whether it has undergone persistent increases in concentration.

A simple method of summarising the tendency for the change in concentration to be associated between three dates is to regress the change in the period 1963–8 on the change in 1958–63, as in chapter 4. The ordinary least-squares regression with $n = 144$ is 0.0426 (0.0746) which is not significantly different from zero. Thus, among the 144 comparable

[1] Products were separated according to whether their predominant buyers were consumers or not. The twelve consumer products identified were: flour confectionery, trailers and caravans, woven carpets, other garments (knitted outerwear), corsets and brassieres, washing machines, overalls and jeans, hats, whisky, detergents, synthetic carpets, and wallpaper.

products over the decade 1958–68 there was no tendency for increases in concentration in the first sub-period 1958–63 to be followed by a corresponding increase in the sub-period 1963–8. The increase in the average level of product concentration in both sub-periods must not be regarded as evidence of *persistent* increases in concentration. At the same time, there is no evidence of a negative regression and thus there was no tendency for an increase in concentration in one period to be corrected by a decrease in the following period.

The corresponding regression of concentration change in 1968–75 on that for 1963–8 for 222 comparable products is −0.0293 (0.0654), which is negative but not significantly different from zero, and adjusting for the different lengths of period, seven and five years, does not alter this conclusion. It would appear that windfall gains and losses of market shares by the largest firms are unlikely to explain changes in concentration over time. In order to gain further insight into the causes of changes in concentration, it is useful to study in more detail those products within the random sample which had increases or decreases in concentration over the period 1958–68.

PRODUCTS WITH INCREASES IN CONCENTRATION 1958–68

Products which displayed a net increase in their concentration ratios over the decade 1958 to 1968 are reviewed in this section with the object of identifying the major forces which increase a product concentration ratio. There were twenty product groups in the random sample with higher concentration in 1968 than in 1958. Seventeen of them experienced concentration increases in both 1958–63 and 1963–8 as shown in table 5.4, although the magnitude of the increases varied between sub-periods and between products.

One hypothesis, that products with contracting markets will tend to have increasing concentration, does not appear to gain much support from a preliminary division of the 27 product groups. Nevertheless, on closer inspection, it becomes apparent that market contraction was an important factor at work in a number of products which had increases in concentration. There were seven products, listed in table 5.2, with increases in concentration and stationary or declining output of which no less than five were in Order XIII (textiles). The period 1958–68 saw a general depression in the old textile industries, associated with the development of new industries producing petroleum-based synthetic fibres. This switch to synthetic fibres affected each of these five products, causing stagnation or contraction with enterprise closures, protective mergers and hence increases in concentration.

The case of the jute industry provides a good example of the impact of

Table 5.4. *Characteristics of products in the random sample with increases in concentration 1958–68*

Percentages

MLH		Concentration ratio			Characteristics[a]
		1958	1963	1968	
Increases in both 1958–63 and 1963–8					
212	Flour confectionery	26.7	51.0	60.1	C, L, M
339(1)	Mining machinery	36.2	42.2	59.1	Cg, L, M
362	Insulated wires and cables	53.3	68.0	81.8	L, M
363	Telephone installations	90.4	94.0	96.4	M
363	Line apparatus	93.9	96.2	99.9	M
368	Washing machines	76.4	85.2	86.9	C
381	Trailers and caravans	37.0	43.5	44.2	C, L, M
412	Flax	38.2	46.8	55.6	Cg, L, M
414(1)	Wool sorting, etc.	39.2	42.5	50.0	Cg, L, M
415	Jute, yarn and cloth	47.7	55.6[b]	68.9	Cg, L, M
417	Other garments (knitted outerwear)	15.0	21.2	33.2	C, L, M
419	Woven carpets	41.2	42.3	57.5	Cg, C, L, M
421(2,3)	Narrow fabrics (non-elastic)	22.5	26.0	31.3	Cg, L
429(1)	Asbestos manufactures	77.4	82.4	86.2	—
444(1)	Heavy overalls and aprons	24.7	26.7[b]	27.4	C, L
446	Hats, caps and millinery	24.0	29.5	36.1	Cg, C, L
449(1)	Corsets and brassieres	30.8	38.0	59.0	C, L, M
Increases in 1958–63 or in 1963–8					
271(2)	Organic chemicals	59.3	64.9	63.2	—
336	Contractors' plant	38.2	38.2	39.7	L, M
471(2)	Builders' woodwork	19.2	18.4	23.0	L, M

SOURCES: As table 5.2.
[a] Cg: contracting; C: consumer goods; L: low initial level of concentration; M: with merger activity.
[b] Ratios in the 1968 Census were: jute 59.2 and heavy overalls 26.0.

man-made fibres and new processes on old textile activities. In the United Kingdom, jute production has been declining since the war. On the demand side factors involved in this contraction were the decline in linoleum sales and in the demand for sacks. The former was partly due to the development of tufted carpets which were substituted for linoleum, while the latter was due to the development of alternative, including oil-based, types of containers. On the other hand, the start of tufted carpet production in the United Kingdom after 1956 gave a temporary boost to jute production as backing for tufted carpets. However, this check to the decline in the trade was only shortlived, and in the period 1963–8 oil-based polypropylene was increasingly substituted for jute in the tufted carpet industry.

Thus in general there existed a problem of surplus capacity in jute production due to the introduction of oil-based substitutes. This problem was exacerbated by the abolition, by the Scottish Court in April 1963, of seven restrictive practices in the industry and by the relaxation of protection against cheap Indian and Pakistani jute goods. The combination of these factors led to a great deal of structural reorganisation in the industry. Mergers and takeovers occurred involving the leading firms in the industry. Inefficient production units were closed down and production concentrated in the most efficient units. Leading firms also diversified into synthetic fibre spinning and, later, polypropylene processing. The increase in concentration by over 21 points in the period 1958–68 reflects these changes.

The cases of wool (sorted, blended, etc.) and flax provide similar examples of old materials and processes being replaced by new ones. Another example of interest, since synthetic carpets will be discussed in the next section, is woven (woollen) carpets. This product group accounted for 81 per cent of all carpet sales by larger establishments in 1958 but only 43 per cent in 1968. This decline was due to the expansion of tufted carpets and also of woven (synthetic) carpets. In absolute terms, employment in the woven (woollen) carpets sub-trade fell 19 per cent in the period 1958–68 due to the substitution of man-made fibres for wool. This decline was an important factor at work in the intensive merger activity which occurred in the industry after 1963.

Contraction of production appears to have been important also in narrow fabrics (non-elastic), in hats, etc. and in mining machinery. The last group provides another example of a decline following the switch to oil products, in this case away from coal. But increases in concentration following from such declines in output should not cause alarm as far as monopoly policy is concerned. First, none of the seven product groups mentioned so far is highly concentrated, with only one (jute) having a concentration ratio above the average for the 27 products in 1968 of 62.0 per cent. Secondly, conditions of falling demand are not usually conducive to the earning of excess profits through the exercise of monopoly power. However, although profits may not be high relative to those in expanding industries, the larger enterprises in a declining market are naturally concerned to cushion *themselves* as far as possible from the effects of lower demand. This often induces them to acquire and close their smaller rivals, a policy with private benefits which may not be desirable from a social point of view. Thirdly, the very fact that output is declining because of the expansion of substitute products based on oil shows that the census definitions of products differ from the economists' concept of a competing group. For example, if it were possible to measure concentration in the textiles competing group as a whole, it is possible that a different picture with regard to concentration change might emerge.

While seven products experienced concentration increases partly as a result of market contraction, another thirteen experienced such increases despite market expansion. The majority of these products, as might be expected, experienced concentration increases predominantly by merger as shown in table 5.2. But other factors also caused concentration to increase in these product groups. One general factor at work in some products was the possibility of economies of scale at plant level. In these cases it could be argued that the increase in enterprise concentration reflected the policies of firms attempting to take advantage of such economies.[1]

It seems likely that potential economies of scale were one of the factors which increased concentration in knitted outerwear. This group had the distinction of having the lowest concentration ratio of all 27 products in 1958 at 15.0 per cent. The hosiery industry as a whole, of which this product group accounted for over 50 per cent of sales in 1968, was regarded by some writers as an example of almost perfect competition. The total number of enterprises in the industry exceeded a thousand in 1958, and the ease of entry was facilitated by an abundance of cheap second-hand knitting machines. At the same time, however, technical developments meant that more efficient, large, automatic knitting machines were available to firms with sufficient capital to invest in them. Such machines would require larger assured markets and would imply both larger enterprises and larger plants. An indication of the latter is given by the fact that the Florence-median plant size for the hosiery industry as a whole increased from 86 to 108 employees between 1958 and 1968, while we know enterprise concentration increased by 18.2 points to 33.2 per cent. However, the reorganisation of hosiery production did not occur solely or primarily in order to gain plant scale-economies. In particular, it appears that forward integration by Courtaulds in order to ensure outlets for its synthetic fibres was a primary cause of increasing concentration in this product group. It is thus not certain that potential plant economies would have had a significant effect on concentration if Courtaulds had not adopted a policy of forward integration by acquisition.

A second product group where plant scale-economies may have been important is organic chemicals. Despite experiencing rapid growth, this product group had above-average concentration (63.2 per cent in 1968) largely as the result of the economies of scale available to it. In 1958 such advantages were not fully realised and the subsequent decade saw the building of larger and larger plants. Although output nearly trebled between 1958 and 1968, concentration still rose by 4 to 5 percentage points. This was due to the tremendous expansion of capacity of the leading producers, particularly ICI at Wilton, Shell at Carrington, and

---

[1] An attempt to measure the average importance of this factor was made in chapter 4, where data on plant sizes at the MLH (three-digit) level were utilised in a multiple regression analysis.

British Hydrocarbon Chemicals at Grangemouth. This expansion of capacity has more than outweighed the tendency for market growth to reduce concentration.

Other examples of product groups where increasing plant size is likely to explain part of the increase in concentration are flour confectionery, asbestos manufactures, electric cables, telephone installations and line apparatus. Although theoretically the ratio of optimal plant size to market size would seem to be an important determinant of enterprise concentration, it is clear from the case studies that this factor was only operative in increasing concentration in some product groups, and even then it represented only part of the explanation. These findings are consistent with the significant but small positive effect of this factor found in the regression analyses carried out in chapter 4 at industry level.

Another important factor making for increases in product concentration over the period 1958–68 was government industrial policy. One of the most notable examples of this during the late 1960s was encouragement to enterprises to merge by the Industrial Reorganisation Corporation (IRC). One field in particular in which the IRC played an important role was electrical engineering, where it encouraged the General Electric Company (GEC)–Associated Electrical Industries (AEI)–English Electric mergers of 1967–8, thus forming one of the largest companies in United Kingdom manufacturing. This was a merger of diversified companies, and was so large that it seems worthwhile to see what effects it had on the concentration of individual product groups in the random sample.

Four products from the electrical engineering industry are in the random sample: insulated wires and cables, telephone installations, line apparatus and washing machines. Telegraph and telephone installations (complete) and line apparatus may be treated together. They are part of a technologically advanced industry (MLH 363) and are dominated by a few large companies. In addition the bulk of sales are to the Post Office, which accepts a policy (formal in the first case, informal in the second) of industry regulation. As can be seen from table 5.4 both product groups had five-enterprise concentration in excess of 90 per cent in 1958 so that the scope for concentration increase was limited. Nevertheless, both groups experienced a 6 points rise, fairly evenly split between the two sub-periods. The GEC–AEI–English Electric mergers were the principal cause of the increases in concentration in the period 1963–8. Mergers between Telephone Manufacturing Company and Pye in 1960, and Plessey–Automatic Telephone and Electric–Ericsson in 1961, were primarily responsible for the increase in 1958–63. In these two product groups, therefore, IRC policies increased concentration.

On the other hand, concentration in washing machines seems to have been little affected by the formation of the GEC giant in 1968. This product group was dominated by Hoover which acted as a price-leader, but AEI–Hotpoint and English Electric were also major producers. In 1966 AEI and EMI (Electrical Musical Industries) joined their washing machine interests to form British Domestic Appliances. The GEC–AEI–English Electric merger undoubtedly formed a large washing machine producer, but the concentration ratio increased only slightly in the period 1963–8. The impact of the mergers was countered by the failure of large producers such as Rolls Razor and Radiation. In addition, if three of the enterprises in the top five merge, the concentration ratio increases, *ceteris paribus*, by the combined market share of the enterprises previously ranked sixth and seventh and they may be relatively small. It is possible that this arithmetic limitation of C_5 also contributed to the small increase in concentration in washing machines in the period 1963–8.

In the remaining electrical engineering product group, insulated wires and cables, the GEC-AEI-English Electric merger had only a limited impact. More important in the 28.5 point concentration rise in the decade 1958–68 appears to have been government policy in abolishing restrictive practices. This product suffered a history of over-capacity. Restriction of competition by output quotas and minimum prices ended after the 1952 Monopolies Commission report,[1] but the Board of Trade supervised minimum prices on rubber, thermoplastic and mains cable. Such supervision was, however, voluntarily terminated in 1959 following the Restrictive Practices legislation, giving rise to price competition and merger activity. Since price and output agreements between separate enterprises were likely to become illegal, there was a direct incentive for the firms with such agreements to merge and resume their previous policies on price and output within one enterprise, where they were legal. Thus there was a wave of acquisition activity by the industry leader British Insulated Callender's Cables (BICC), by the second ranking firm AEI, and by several other large producers. Against this background, the activities of the IRC were less important in this product group.

The 1965 Restrictive Trade Practices Act appears to have had an effect in encouraging mergers and increasing concentration in several other product groups in our random sample. We have already mentioned the case of jute, where action by the Scottish Court in 1963 was a factor on the supply side which encouraged industry reorganisation. The abolition of price and discount agreements in the carpet industry by the Restrictive Practices Court in 1959 was also a factor in the reorganisation of this industry. While on the one hand, it led to merger activity in woven carpets, on the other, it encouraged experiments in synthetic carpets, which

---

[1] Monopolies Commission, *Report on the Supply of Insulated Electric Wires and Cables*, London, HMSO, 1952.

hitherto had been treated as cheap low-quality products under the price agreement of the Carpet Federation. While other factors were at work in each of these cases, it seems reasonable to infer that the abolition of restrictive practices did on balance increase concentration.

The other particular feature which is of some interest in the period 1958–68 is the part played by forward integration of firms in increasing concentration. This was prevalent in the textile and clothing industries, where, as has been stressed, the development of synthetic fibres caused important changes. In particular, Courtaulds integrated forward in several product groups in order to guarantee outlets for its man-made fibres. Thus, for example, it bought its way into corsets and brassieres in 1959 with the acquisition of Gossards, and into knitted goods in 1963 with the acquisition of the largest firm, Bairns-Wear. Courtaulds also took over the largest firm in elastics, Clutsom-Penn International, in 1968. This policy inevitably provoked response. For example, when continued acquisitions by Courtaulds in corsets and brassieres made it the third largest producer by 1968, behind Playtex and Silhouette, smaller firms (for example, Spirella–Leethems and Wood Barstow–Slix) merged in order to remain independent. In knitted goods also, smaller firms merged to protect themselves not only from Courtaulds but also from Coats Patons and from Joseph Dawson (Holdings), both of which followed Courtaulds in integrating forward into the hosiery industry. Courtaulds' policy therefore caused large concentration increases in traditionally non-concentrated industries.

Another example of forward integration is in flour confectionery. In this product group, part of the large concentration increase of 33.4 points was a by-product of the forward integration of millers, Ranks and Spillers, into bread production. This provoked response from Associated British Foods and the Cooperative Wholesale Society and led to a wholesale scramble for bread-making plant; and, inevitably, considerable cake-making plant was acquired in the process. In addition, 1962 saw the diversification of Cadbury and United Biscuits into the fast expanding sector of packaged cakes.

Thus forward integration must be added to the other factors which promoted increases in product concentration in the decade 1958 to 1968, namely market contraction, plant economies of scale, government industrial policy and, paradoxically, the abolition of restrictive trade practices.

PRODUCTS WITH DECREASES IN CONCENTRATION 1958–68

Seven product groups in table 5.2 had lower sales concentration ratios in 1968 than in 1958. This section discusses these products with a view to identifying the important factors which tended to reduce product concentration.

Table 5.5. *Characteristics of products in the random sample with decreases in concentration 1958–68*

Percentages

MLH		Concentration ratio			Characteristics[a]
		1958	1963	1968	
239(1)	Whisky	96.1	94.2	91.0	E, C, H
275	Detergents	90.4	84.5	79.9	E, C, H
339(9)	Pulp-making machinery	84.0	93.8	83.3	H
341(1)	Boilers	69.8	60.3	61.7	H
419	Synthetic carpets	65.6	55.0	54.4	E, C, H
431(2)	Fellmongery	46.1	42.7	42.2	E
484(1)	Wallpaper	91.6	95.1[b]	89.7	E, C, H

SOURCES: As table 5.2.

[a] E: expanding; C: consumer good; H: high initial level of concentration.

[b] Ratio in 1968 Census: 95.6.

The first point to note is that the separation of these seven product groups from the others is to some extent arbitrary. As table 5.5 indicates, only four of them had persistent concentration falls. The experience of the other three (pulp-making machinery, boilers and wallpaper) was mixed, so that their inclusion in this section is in part determined by the particular years chosen for comparison. Three additional product groups (organic chemicals, contractors' plant and builders' woodwork) also had a mixed experience but over the period 1958–68 had a net increase in concentration, so that they have not been considered here. Secondly, the concentration decrease in the seven product groups varies from marginal in pulp-making machinery (0.7 points) to substantial in synthetic carpets (11.2 points). It will be shown that these net change figures are in certain cases misleading, but here it is sufficient to note the diversity of experience they contain.

In spite of the limitations of the data, these seven products suffice to indicate the forces reducing concentration. Two of the most systematic of these forces are shown in table 5.5, namely initial high concentration levels and market growth.

Only one of the seven product groups (fellmongery) had a concentration ratio below the average for all 27 products in 1958. The average concentration of the seven products was 77.7 per cent in 1958, with three of them (whisky, detergents and wallpaper) having concentration ratios exceeding 90 per cent. Thus there is a prima facie case in favour of the argument that there is a tendency for the highest concentration ratios to decrease.

Wallpaper may be considered as a possible example of this tendency. The share of the five top enterprises in sales of this product was 91.6 per cent in 1958, largely reflecting the four fifths share of the market held by Wall Paper Manufacturers (WPM).[1] In 1899, on its formation by the voluntary amalgamation of 31 wallpaper firms, WPM claimed 98 per cent of the market. Throughout this century there has been a tendency for this position to be eroded by continual new entry into what is an industry with low entry barriers. Working against this tendency has been WPM's acquisition policy – time and again buying out its new competitors. The concentration rise in the period 1958–63 largely reflects the dominance of this latter force. After 1963, however, the long-run tendency towards concentration decrease again asserted itself, in a period of expanding production of vinyl wall coverings, when an adverse Monopolies Commission report and the takeover of WMP by Reed Paper in 1965 severely limited its acquisitions. Indeed, the Monopolies Commission recommended that further acquisitions should not be allowed without the consent of the Board of Trade. Clearly the erosion of the high level of concentration in the wallpaper product group has not been dramatic since 1899, and perhaps little reliance can be placed on reducing high concentration levels unless there are low barriers to entry and unless the acquisition activity by leading firms is restricted.

Another example of a decrease from high concentration levels is whisky. This product group has been dominated by Distillers since its acquisition of Buchanan-Dewar and John Walker in 1925, which brought its share of United Kingdom whisky production to 80 per cent. Despite exporting three quarters of its production, it had about three quarters of the domestic market in 1959–60. The fall in C_5 from 96 per cent in 1958 to 91 per cent in 1968 was probably due to a fall in Distillers' share of the domestic market at a time of fast market growth. Part of the fall was due to the expansion of other leading whisky producers, but part was due to the policy of major brewers in promoting their own brands of whisky (some of which they produced themselves) in their tied outlets. Thus the entry of brewers into production had the effect of reducing the Distillers' monopoly in a way that Distillers could do little to counter. In this case the acquisition activity of the market leader was limited by the fact that new entrants were themselves very large companies diversifying into the industry.

In addition to high initial concentration and limitations on merger activity, it seems likely that growth is a factor which tends to decrease concentration. In table 5.5 five of the seven products with decreases in

---

[1] The Monopolies Commission gave WPM's market share as 80 per cent in 1961 (*Report on the Supply of Wallpaper*, p. 41). In other years its share was subject to large variations which in part reflected its acquisition policy.

concentration experienced market growth. In the case of synthetic carpets, market growth appears to have been the predominant factor tending to decrease concentration.

Synthetic carpets, or to use its census title 'other carpets, carpeting and floor rugs', comprises a collection of residual categories of carpets, of which the most important, accounting for 79 per cent of sales in 1968, is synthetic woven carpets. The large increase in wool prices in the period 1956–60 encouraged experimentation with synthetic fibre blends which resulted in a large expansion of the output of synthetic carpets. The abolition of the Carpet Federation's price agreement in 1959 further stimulated this trend, so that between 1958 and 1968 there occurred a sevenfold expansion in terms of employment and a fourteenfold expansion in terms of gross output. This tremendous growth in this new product area was the major cause of the large fall of 11.2 percentage points in five-enterprise concentration in this group. It is a classic case of a new product experiencing rapid growth and concentration decline. But most of the decline in concentration occurred in 1958–63, as shown in table 5.5. In the period 1963–8, however, the market leaders were able more or less to maintain their positions, by internal growth in the case of John Crossley-Carpet Trades, Homfray, and Blackwood Morton, and by acquisition in the case of Bond Worth. In this example the concentration reduction due to the expansion of a new product seems to have been relatively shortlived.

The examples used so far suggest that market growth, high initial concentration levels, low entry barriers, and limitations on acquisition activity tend to decrease concentration. However, these examples have been limited to the four consumer goods in the sub-sample of seven product groups. The evidence on producer goods is not so satisfactory. Fellmongery may be distinguished from the two machine-producing industries in our sub-sample for it is a technologically primitive industry with sales in 1968 of only £10.5 million. Table 5.5 shows that the decrease in concentration occurred in the sub-period 1958–63. Over these five years net output more than doubled, employment increased by nearly 40 per cent, but both fell between 1963 and 1968. The decrease in concentration fostered by market growth was virtually confined to 1958 to 1963. Thus this case does not lead to different conclusions from the consumer-goods cases.

For the capital-goods industries the case is different. The marginal decline in concentration in pulp, paper and board-making machinery occurred despite a substantial market decline which reduced the number of producers. The observed fall in concentration is primarily due to the dates chosen for comparison and principally reflects the rise and decline of one firm, Black-Clawson International, which entered the industry in 1957. On the other hand, the concentration ratio is a rather redundant concept in the product group boilers and boilerhouse plant. About three quarters of its production takes the form of giant boilers sold to the electricity generating boards. Conventional boilers are primarily produced by members of the Water Tube Boilermakers Association, who tender by agreement, while consortia are formed to tender for nuclear contracts. The trade is clearly very closely regulated, the concentration fall in the period 1958–68 probably being associated with the allocation of several generating board orders to non-association members.

Evidence on capital-goods industries is not so clear cut as on consumer-goods industries. Such as it is, it gives rise to the tentative suggestion that concentration ratios may be typically less meaningful in such industries, because the lumpiness of their output flows may often produce different market shares depending on the year being considered. It may be that systematic relationships between concentration change and other variables differ substantially between consumers' and capital goods. This also illustrates the advantages to be obtained from using case studies in addition to statistical analysis in establishing the plausibility of these relationships; on the average the dichotomy between producers' and consumers' goods may have no effect on changes in concentration, but the examples of capital goods show that changes in their concentration ratios differ in character from those of consumers' goods because of the discrete nature of their output flow.

CONCLUSIONS

This chapter has discussed the reasons for changes in product concentration over the period 1958 to 1968. Special reference is made to the role of mergers in increasing concentration at the product level, but other factors at work are forward integration, market contraction, plant economies of scale, and government policy in the form of the IRC and the Restrictive Trade Practices Act. The factors making for decreases in product concentration include market growth, high initial concentration levels, low entry barriers and limitations on acquisitions of enterprises. These conclusions are based on a series of case studies in a previous National Institute Occasional Paper rather than on regression analyses. Few of the factors listed above can be measured at the product (four-digit) level and so the usual regression analyses are inappropriate.

The findings that mergers were primarily responsible for increases in concentration in fourteen products out of a sample of 27, and that the average increase in concentration in these fourteen products was 15.4 percentage points (compared with the 7.8 percentage points increase in average concentration in the six products with concentration increases without mergers), indicate that mergers had very important effects on the increase in average concentration over the decade 1958–68. It is not possible to estimate these effects with much precision but our results, based on the case studies, suggest that mergers were responsible for about half of the average increase in product concentration from 1958 to 1968. Indeed, merger activity accelerated between 1963 and 1968 and increased concentration in more products than it did in the earlier period 1958–63. These results refer to average changes in *product* concentration ratios and must be distinguished from the analyses of variance in chapter 4, which refer to variations between *industries* of logarithmic changes in concentration ratios.

It has been shown in chapters 2 and 3 that there has been a tendency for the *average* product concentration ratio to increase steadily since 1958 and for *average* industrial concentration to increase since 1951 and probably since the first measurements were available in 1935. However, this persistent increase of average concentration must not be used to support hypotheses of increasing concentration of capital because of economies of scale and the like. If this were true, there would be persistent increases in concentration in *each* of the individual product groups concerned, and this does not happen. The continuous increase in average concentration occurs, even though individual concentration ratios show a less systematic pattern, because the increases outweigh the decreases over time. The tendency for concentration increases to persist may be measured by the regression of the change in each product for 1963–8 on the corresponding change for 1958–63, using the 144 comparable products in table 3.3. This regression was estimated at 0.0426 (0.0746), which is positive but not significantly different from zero. Similarly the regression of the change in concentration of 222 comparable products for 1968–75 on the corresponding change for 1963–8 was −0.0293 (0.0654), which is also not significantly different from zero. Thus, whilst it is true that average concentration increased in the period 1958–68 and that for 21 of the 27 products concentration changed in the same direction in the two sub-periods distinguished, it cannot be concluded that the *magnitudes* of the change were correlated in consecutive periods. Rather it would seem that there is very little scope for predicting future concentration changes for individual products from previous changes for those products.

Furthermore, dynamic factors are also important *within* individual product groups. Is there any tendency for the same enterprises to increase their market shares in consecutive periods? Or is the continuous increase in concentration in the seventeen products in table 5.4 primarily due to the entry of new firms into the top ranks, ousting former leaders, as a result of their superior efficiency? The Census of Production statistics do not provide answers to such questions: case studies can. Moreover, the formal statistical analysis is necessarily confined to comparable products and yet, as a result of its dynamic nature, the industrial composition of manufacturing is continuously changing, so that those products which are comparable over a long period tend to be those which are not new nor rapidly changing in character. Thus new substitute products, which are a continued threat to existing monopolies or oligopolies, tend to be excluded from the regression equations. These qualifications to the statistical analysis above, which relate to the dynamics of business concentration, must always be borne in mind.

EFFECTS OF CONCENTRATION ON
PRICES, PROFITABILITY, WAGES AND EFFICIENCY

INTRODUCTION

A common criticism of monopoly capitalism is that increasing industrial concentration leads to unduly low outputs and excessively high prices and profits. This criticism is based on standard theoretical models which are taught throughout universities in the western world. In times of price inflation and output stagnation it is especially tempting to extend government policies to promote competition in the hope that this will help to reduce the rate of inflation and to increase the growth of output. However, there are important counter-arguments. Practical businessmen emphasise the economies of scale, the new techniques, the greater stability of output (and hence employment) which are sometimes associated with increases in industrial concentration and they may oppose policies which intensify competition. They claim that their enterprises must be larger in order to compete in the international market with large American or German rivals. They are often supported by trade union leaders, who naturally welcome any increased stability of employment and any increased wages yielded by less competitive industries. Thus competition policies based on standard microeconomic theory are not necessarily adopted by the government, even if the weight of expert opinion is in their favour.

The compromise reached in the United Kingdom is to treat each case on its merits: to reject the proposition that increased competition is always desirable and to compare the advantages and disadvantages of existing (or potential) monopolies and tight oligopolies in a case-by-case approach. This makes good sense, but it will be many years before such an approach yields enough information to support a general conclusion on the effects of increases in industrial concentration on prices, profitability, wages and efficiency. Indeed, it may never be possible to reach general conclusions on the effects of increases in industrial concentration from such case studies alone, because by the time the number of cases is large enough to be representative of all oligopolies, the earlier studies are out of date and require further investigation.

Thus the economic research worker has to supplement case studies of individual industries with statistical analyses of large numbers of industries in order to assess average relationships between concentration and prices, profitability, wages and efficiency. This statistical evidence is reviewed in the next four sections of this chapter, but it must not be thought that only these four relationships are important. On the contrary, it is possible that increasing industrial concentration is associated with, for example, changes in the quality of products which cannot be measured statistically. The speed of delivery, the quality of after-sales service and the readiness to meet customers' special requirements may be better in more competitive industries, but there are no industrial statistics on these important components of economic performance and so they cannot be correlated with concentration. Thus the statistical analysis of this chapter is merely part of the story, albeit an important part.

PRICES AND INDUSTRIAL CONCENTRATION

The prices of the products of manufacturing industry depend on the interaction of demand and supply. Most manufacturing industries produce intermediate goods which are purchased by other industries to use as inputs into the final products sold to consumers. The demand for intermediate goods is derived from this final demand and may not be very sensitive to advertising or even to relative prices. In addition, some manufacturing industries are heavily dependent on export markets and thus the demand for their output also depends on the exchange rate.

The forces affecting prices from the supply side are equally complex. Wages and salaries, raw-material costs, fuel and transport charges, indirect taxes and employers' insurance contributions would all tend to influence the prices of the output of a manufacturing industry. Additional influences could come from labour productivity, from technical progress, from the degree of capacity utilisation and from changes in the target profit-margin or the level of profitability which firms regard as normal. Again, some industries are heavily dependent on imported raw materials and their prices could be influenced by changes in the exchange rate.

The problem is to assess the importance of a single variable, industrial concentration, in the complicated network of forces which influence prices. In order to do this it is necessary to formulate a model of the determination of price changes in manufacturing industry which is inevitably a simplification. This task is considerably eased by the balanced survey of the extensive literature on this subject by Silberston, who concludes that for manufacturing industry 'the main influence leading to price changes is a change in the level of costs, especially when this is general in its effects'.[1]

---

[1] A. Silberston ('Price behaviour of firms', *Economic Journal*, vol. 80, 1970, p. 569) allows demand to influence price indirectly through changes in costs. We accept this qualification, which implies that the cost variable on the right-hand side of our equation in table 6.1 may also be reflecting demand conditions.

This judgement enables us to use one of the standard econometric pricing equations which are generally based on costs rather than on demand. Thus we postulate that for each industry the proportionate change in its average price depends on the average proportionate changes in its wages, labour productivity and other costs (mainly raw materials, fuel and packaging). In addition, the proportionate change in the industry's concentration ratio and the average *level* of concentration are included in turn as possible explanatory variables. The sources and methods used to obtain the data are described in appendix 6A.[1]

Table 6.1. *Regressions of price changes on cost changes and concentration across 121 industries, 1963–8*

	Ratio 1968/1963		Equation number[a]	
	Mean	Standard deviation	(1)	(2)
Prices	1.1409	0.1257	..	..
Wages	1.3913	0.0596	0.2871[b]	0.3138[b]
			(0.1295)	(0.1324)
Labour productivity	1.2562	0.1571	−0.3056[b]	−0.3118[b]
			(0.0616)	(0.0619)
Other costs	1.1734	0.2568	0.2497[b]	0.2448[b]
			(0.0361)	(0.0362)
Concentration	1.1144	0.2217	0.0446	0.0004[c]
			(0.0331)	(0.0032)
$\bar{R}^2$			0.603	0.596

SOURCES: See appendix 6A.
[a] Standard errors in brackets.
[b] Significantly different from zero at 5 per cent level.
[c] Coefficient and standard error are multiplied by 10.

The results are summarised in table 6.1. The proportionate change in each variable is measured by the ratio of its value in 1968 to its value in 1963. The period 1963–8 was chosen originally because the 1968 concentration ratios were the most recent available. More recent concentration ratios are available now, but price controls have become so important in recent years that regression analysis is less likely to reveal any relationship between price changes and concentration changes. Even the results for 1963–8 may have been affected by price controls after the National Board for Prices and Incomes was set up in 1965. However, we do not believe this to be the case because similar results were obtained from

[1] In view of the controversy between L. Phlips ('Business pricing policies and inflation – some evidence from EEC countries', *Journal of Industrial Economics*, vol. 18, 1969) and H. N. Ross ('Illusions in testing for administered prices', *Journal of Industrial Economics*, vol. 21, 1973) it must be stressed that our specification is not tautological; the profit mark-up on costs is excluded.

using data for 55 industries in 1958–63. The size of the sample for 1963–8 was determined by the data available; it was possible to measure changes in prices for 121 industries which were comparable over these five years.

The price, wage, labour productivity and concentration variables are familiar enough, but a brief comment on 'other costs' may be helpful at this stage. The increase in these depends on the increase in the prices of these inputs and the change in their quantities. We have corrected for changes in their quantities by dividing the proportionate change in other costs by the proportionate change in the real net output of each industry. The implicit assumption is that this method of removing the quantity change leaves as a residual the pure price change of inputs other than labour. Thus the first column in table 6.1 shows that these prices increased by about 17.3 per cent over the period 1963–8 compared with an average increase in output prices of just over 14 per cent. This column also gives the mean ratios of wages, labour productivity, and concentration, which increased 39.1, 25.6 and 11.4 per cent respectively. The second column measures the variation of these variables across the 121 industries. It can be seen that proportionate changes in wages vary very little across industries.[1]

Estimates of two forms of equation are given in table 6.1. Equation (1) includes the proportionate change in concentration, while equation (2) includes the average of the 1963 and 1968 concentration ratios for each industry. In each column it can be seen that the regression coefficient on the concentration measure is not significantly different from zero. That is, neither the average level nor the proportionate change in concentration had any significant effect on price changes over the period 1963–8. The important determinants of price increases were wage increases, changes in the productivity of labour and changes in the prices of raw materials, fuel, etc. All these variables had significant regression coefficients with appropriate signs. There is no evidence to support the hypothesis that industries with a high level of concentration or with a large increase in concentration tend to have large price increases.[2]

---

[1] This low dispersion is consistent with the widely held view that part of the inflation experienced over this period was caused by wage increases in 'key industries', possibly with relatively high productivity increases, being followed by wage increases in the remaining and less critical industries as the result of trade unions' successful attempts to maintain differentials. This explanation may or may not be true, but table 6.1 makes it clear that the standard deviation of wages was well below that of labour productivity and this result is also consistent with the 'key industry' or structural explanation of wage inflation. Empirical tests of the 'key industry hypothesis' for the period 1958–67 are reported by J. Eatwell, J. Llewellyn and R. Tarling, 'Money wage inflation in industrial countries', *Review of Economic Studies*, vol. 41, 1974. See also G. Maynard and W. van Ryckeghem, *A World of Inflation*, London, Batsford, 1976.

[2] This conclusion is based on medium-term changes over the five-year period 1963–8. S. Domberger, 'Price adjustment and market structure', *Economic Journal*, vol. 89, 1979, has recently claimed that the

This hypothesis is usually advanced by the administered price inflation school of thought and members of this school may object to our conclusion on the grounds that the regressions in table 6.1 relate to all 121 industries with a wide range of concentration levels and changes, whereas only those industries with very high levels of, or high changes in, concentration could be expected to impose above-average price increases. There is some threshold level of concentration which has to be reached before the administered price hypothesis is relevant. This argument, formulated by Blair[1] among others, is important and merits separate investigation.

Between 1963 and 1968 the average proportionate increase in concentration was 11 per cent. Table 6.2 arrays fourteen industries which

Table 6.2. *Proportionate changes in prices and extreme changes in concentration, 1963–8*

Percentages

| MLH | | Increase 1963–8 | |
		Concentration	Prices
334	Industrial engines	35.4	12.5
349	General mechanical engineering	31.8	15.1
354	Scientific and industrial instruments	50.0	13.1
396	Jewellery and precious metals	39.4	48.0
412	Spinning and doubling	34.4	19.1
413	Weaving of cotton, etc.	107.1	16.1
422(1)	Household textiles	42.9	12.6
423	Textile finishing	32.2	7.4
444	Overalls, etc.	46.7	10.3
445	Dresses, lingerie, etc.	68.4	7.6
449(1,3,4)	Corsets, etc.	71.4	9.0
461	Bricks, fireclay, etc.	48.2	10.6
462	Pottery	105.0	17.8
471	Timber	57.1	22.6

SOURCES: As table 6.1.

level of concentration, but not the change in this level, has a positive effect on the speed of adjustment of prices to cost increases in the *short term*. He used quarterly time series data on a non-random sample of 21 industries over the period 1963–8. Nine of the sample are engineering industries, which are thought to have lower than average speeds of price adjustment to cost increases. Using Domberger's estimated speeds of adjustment, with the concentration ratios for 1968 in chapter 2 and a dummy variable taking values of one for the nine engineering industries and zero for the remaining twelve, we confirmed that there is a small but significant effect of concentration on speed of price adjustment, $\bar{R}^2 = 0.30$. However, when the dummy variable is excluded $\bar{R}^2 = 0.025$, so the claim that engineering prices are a special case is crucial to Domberger's results. K. Coutts, W. Godley and W. Nordhaus, *Industrial Pricing in the United Kingdom*, Cambridge University Press, 1978, p. 40, found that their two engineering industrial groups had longer production periods than the other five industrial groups they considered (although the textiles group was a close third) and this result provides some support for Domberger's dichotomy.
[1] J. M. Blair, *Economic Concentration, Structure, Behavior and Public Policy*, New York, Harcourt, Brace, Jovanovich, 1972.

had extreme increases in concentration of 30 per cent or over, seven of them in the textile and clothing Orders. The average increase in prices in the 121 industries of table 6.1 was 14 per cent over the period 1963 to 1968. Table 6.2 shows that only six of the fourteen industries (MLH 349, 396, 412, 413, 462 and 471) had price increases above 14 per cent. Again, table 6.3 shows that of eleven industries with average *levels* of concentration in 1963 and 1968 of 80 per cent or more, only four (MLH 240, 279(3), 279(7) and 380) had price increases in excess of the average increase of 14 per cent.

Table 6.3. *Proportionate changes in prices and extreme average levels of concentration, 1963–8*

Percentages

MLH		Concentration level	Change in prices
216	Sugar	97.0	−4.4
229(1)	Margarine	92.0	6.9
240	Tobacco	97.5	27.9
278	Fertilizers	82.0	9.6
279(3)	Explosives, etc.	85.0	16.0
279(7)	Photographic chemicals	91.0	17.6
363	Telephone apparatus	89.0	11.7
380	Wheeled tractor manufacturing	92.0	19.7
411	Production of man-made fibres	99.5	−13.5
429(1)	Asbestos manufactures	80.0	11.5
464	Cement	92.5	9.0

SOURCES: As table 6.1.

Finally, table 6.4 shows nine further industries with high average concentration (70 per cent and over) which also had increasing concentration in 1963–8. Their price increases are also shown. It can be seen

Table 6.4. *Proportionate changes in prices, high average and increasing levels of concentration, 1963–8*

Percentages

MLH		Concentration 1963–8		Price change
		Average level	Increase	
239(2)	British wines, cider and perry	79	2.6	42.2
277	Dyestuffs and pigments	75	—	14.0
279(6)	Surgical bandages, etc.	78.5	1.3	5.2
334	Industrial engines	76.5	35.4	12.5
352	Watches and clocks	79.5	3.8	12.5
362	Insulated wires and cables	77.5	12.3	50.2
382	Motor cycles, pedal cycles, etc.	78	13.7	8.5
395	Cans and metal boxes	73.5	4.2	4.8
469(1)	Abrasives	77	11.0	10.9

SOURCES: As table 6.1.

that only two of these nine had price increases which exceeded the average of 14 per cent, namely MLH 239(2), British wines, cider and perry, and MLH 362, insulated wires and cables. In addition, MLH 277 was marginal with a price increase of 14 per cent.

All the industries in table 6.3 except MLH 279(7), photographic chemicals, had constant or increasing concentration ratios. Thus no table provides any evidence to support the hypothesis that extremely high levels of, or extremely high increases in, concentration are associated with faster increases in prices. Moreover, detailed tests were conducted using the residuals of regression equation (1) in table 6.1 after excluding the concentration variable from the right-hand side, and these confirm the visual impression that there is no evidence of a non-linear effect of concentration on price changes.[1]

While it is possible to find examples such as MLH 362, insulated wires and cables, where an industry with a high level and a large increase in concentration has had a large increase in prices, it is also possible to find counter-examples, such as MLH 469(1), abrasives, where the price increase was below average. When the large sample of 121 industries is studied or when the analysis is confined to the concentrated industries, the conclusion is the same: the increase in prices is not influenced by industrial concentration and is primarily dependent on input prices and labour productivity. Government policies to reduce industrial concentration are unlikely, therefore, to have any effect on the general price level. This conclusion relates to industrial performance *on the average*: it is still possible that *a particular* industry increased its prices by more than the average as the result of its market power.

One possible reason why proportionate changes in concentration have no effect on price changes is that the highly concentrated industries were able to obtain higher levels of prices in the distant past, when the oligopolies were formed, but since then they have merely maintained their price differentials. The introduction of anti-monopoly legislation may have curbed any tendency to increase price differentials. This possibility cannot be investigated directly by comparing price levels in industries with different degrees of concentration, but it can be studied indirectly by comparing the price–cost margins of industries with different concentration ratios. If oligopolies have been able to maintain, but unable to increase, the difference between their prices and those of more competitive industries, we should expect the level of the price–cost margin, but not the proportionate change in that margin, to depend on concentration. The

---

[1] These residuals reflect the proportionate changes in prices after the effects of wages, labour productivity, and other costs have been removed. When plotted against concentration, they provide no evidence of linear or non-linear correlation. Thus there is no evidence of a structural break producing a positive correlation for high levels of concentration.

relationship between this margin and the level and changes in concentration is considered in the next section.

PROFITABILITY AND INDUSTRIAL CONCENTRATION

Most of the studies of the relationship between profitability and industrial concentration have been made by American economists using American data. The limited amount of work on British data is surveyed elsewhere and this survey need not be repeated here.[1] The definition of an industry's profit is determined by the data used, which are usually derived from the Census of Production. This is important because the difference between the census net output or value added and the census sum of wages and salaries gives a measure of gross profit which includes not only depreciation but also advertising and other selling costs, including transport costs. Thus the definition of profit derived from Census of Production sources is far removed from any of the accounting definitions in common use.

The denominators used in these studies are sales (census gross output), value added or capital. The value of sales is affected by raw-material prices, by indirect taxes, by subsidies, and by the degree of vertical integration. For example, two enterprises may have the same profit and the same value added but may record different total sales because the first enterprise, being less integrated, allows its constituent companies or plants to charge market prices for output transferred between them, whereas the second enterprise allows only nominal or even zero prices for such transfers and thereby has lower total sales. Clearly, changes in the degree of integration, in raw-material prices and in the other variables mentioned, would have a statistical effect on the percentage of profits on sales which would not be relevant to the relationship between the degree of monopoly and level of profitability.[2] Consequently, the denominator of value added is to be preferred.

The denominator of value added was used by Hart and Morgan in their comparison of profitability and concentration. In a log-linear regression they found that the concentration ratio appeared to have a small positive effect ($R^2 = 0.094$) on the share of census profit in value added but that this effect disappeared when the advertising–sales ratio and the variable measuring the capital–labour ratio were introduced as further explanatory variables.[3] The significance of these variables is in part due to the fact that

---

[1] P. E. Hart and R. Clarke, 'Profit margins, wages and oligopoly – a survey of the evidence for the UK' (University of Reading Discussion Paper in Economics, series A, no. 108).

[2] The effects of using different denominators is illustrated by two examples, in the brewing and tobacco industries in 1968, in Hart and Clarke, 'Profit margins, wages and oligopoly'.

[3] P. E. Hart and E. Morgan, 'Market structure and economic performance in the United Kingdom', *Journal of Industrial Economics*, vol. 25, 1977. A similar result in fact occurred when a series of linear regressions was used.

advertising expenditure and depreciation already appear in the numerator of the profitability measure so that it is not surprising that the explanatory variables reflecting advertising and capital intensity had significant statistical effects on the dependent variable. When such effects are removed, as they must be, there is no significant association between profitability and concentration.

Four other explanatory variables were added in turn to measure the effects of imports, demand, entry barriers and the number of enterprises on profitability. The import variable did not contribute to the explanation of variations in profitability across industries. It is possible that the ratio of imports to domestic sales of the whole industry does not reflect the degree of competition from imports. After all, it is the threat of imports, or import potential, which would tend to prevent price–cost margins from becoming unduly large. Again, the aggregation of *all* imported products for a whole industry may not reveal the intensity of competition from some imported products classified in that industry.[1] The logarithm of the number of enterprises had a small negative effect on the logarithm of profitability, but this effect was not robust: it did not hold when a similar regression was estimated for 1971. The important explanatory variables for 1968 and 1971 were the advertising–sales ratio and the capital–labour ratio but, because their numerators appeared in the dependent variable, little weight can be attached to this particular statistical result.

The most that can be claimed as a result of the significant effect of the number of enterprises is that oligopolistic structure makes some contribution to variations in levels of profitability between industries as predicted by standard theory, but its importance is probably small compared with all the other systematic and stochastic factors influencing profitability.

No doubt examples of a positive effect of concentration on profitability in some industries can be found but there are always equivalent counter-examples.[2] It is unlikely that any large representative sample of industries will reveal a general association between profitability and concentration because the relationship between economic performance and market structure is very complex. The usual regression analyses performed to ascertain the relationship between market structure and economic performance are at worst mongrel-type equations: at best they are the reduced forms of partial models from which variables such as the price-elasticity of demand, risk, and trade union pressure are excluded.

---

[1] For many industries, imports take the form of inputs (raw materials, components, semi-manufactured goods, or even fully manufactured goods) into domestic firms' production. Thus we should expect an industry cross-section regression of the profits–sales ratios on imports–sales ratios to yield a negative regression coefficient because imports appear in the denominator of the dependent variable, even though the regression of profits–net output on imports–sales is not significantly different from zero.

[2] See Hart and Clarke, 'Profit margins, wages and oligopoly'.

Unfortunately, in order to construct a simultaneous equations model with prices, wages, profit-margins and concentration as endogenous variables, and entry barriers, imports, etc. as exogenous variables, it is necessary to obtain the required data from different sources and this restricts the number of observations so severely that the maximum sample of comparable industries available cannot be regarded as being representative. Thus in practice investigations of the complex relationship between economic performance and market structure in the United Kingdom must lean heavily on single-equation regression analysis. This may be the explanation of why concentration has insignificant regression coefficients, but this is not our view.

There is certainly no evidence to support the belief that the more monopolised industries are more profitable or have high increases in prices. However, there remains the possibility that one of the reasons for these results is that labour absorbs part of the potential monopoly profit in the form of higher wages. This is considered in the next section.

WAGES AND INDUSTRIAL CONCENTRATION

It seems reasonable to suppose that wages tend to be higher in the more concentrated industries, assuming that labour is not perfectly mobile between industries with different concentration ratios, otherwise wages would tend to be equalised. In a world where wages are determined by bilateral bargaining between trade unions and employers, the negotiated wage is likely to increase with union power, *ceteris paribus*. For any given level of union power, employers in the more concentrated industries are likely to concede higher wages than those in competitive industries; they may feel morally obliged to share any monopoly profit with their employees, they may wish to avoid public censure or government intervention which may follow the publication of high profit figures, or they may be less cost-conscious than employers in more competitive industries. In particular they may be more prepared to pay higher wages in order to buy industrial peace, especially when excessive wage bills act as a barrier to the entry of new firms.

Finally, to reinforce this tendency, union pressure is likely to be stronger in the more concentrated industries. There are many possible reasons for this. Where high concentration goes hand in hand with high profits there is a direct incentive for the trade unions concerned to become more militant in attempts to remove the excess monopoly profit by increasing wages. In principle they could bargain for reductions in prices in order to remove the excess profit. While this would increase their product-wages, there is no guarantee that other unions in other industries with similar excess profits would react in the same way, and the risk that their members' real wages would not be increased is too great for any individual union to bargain for price reductions, rather than for money-wage increases, to remove excess profits of monopoly. Furthermore, it has been shown in chapter 4 that high concentration is associated with large plants; these tend to produce large units in trade union organisations and it is likely that the economies of scale of union organisation include the greater capacity to disrupt production on a wide scale which breeds greater militancy. Coupled with this is the widely held belief, which dates back to Adam Smith, that the large-scale operations associated with highly concentrated industries generate feelings of alienation among the employees and this alienation makes them more militant.[1]

Many studies have included the degree of industrial concentration among the determinants of wages but most of the regression estimates are highly equivocal and the measures of concentration used less reliable than the concentration ratios estimated in chapter 2.[2] We therefore decided to estimate new regressions, and it will be seen that our results are similar to those of Metcalf, Nickell and Richardson[3] even though we used different data, different equations and different estimation techniques.

Details of the variables used in the regressions and their sources are given in appendix 6A. Hourly earnings data are potentially the most useful for our purpose because not only do they relate to full-time adult male manual workers, but also allowance is made for overtime, shift-work, and bonus and commission payments, as well as holiday and sick pay. Hence, these data approximate more closely to the male manual basic wage than either weekly earnings or annual earnings. Against these advantages however, there must be placed two disadvantages of hourly earnings data. The first is that the earliest year for which the data are available is 1970, whilst most of our other variables refer to 1968. And the second is that even for 1970 the data are not sufficiently disaggregated for our purposes, so that for just under half of our sample it was necessary to use values of this variable which relate to a group of industries of which the industry under consideration was a part.

We have used two alternative measures of the effect of union power on earnings. TUA, the number of working days lost per thousand employees averaged over the period 1966–8, corresponds to the variable U used by

[1] An interesting discussion on this subject may be found in K. D. George, R. McNabb and J. Shorey, 'The size of the work unit and labour market behaviour', *British Journal of Industrial Relations*, vol. 15, 1977. A fascinating relationship between strikes and the size of plant is formulated by S. J. Prais, 'The strike-proneness of large plants in Britain', *Journal of the Royal Statistical Society* (series A), vol. 141, part 3, 1978.
[2] See Hart and Clarke, 'Profit margins, wages and oligopoly'.
[3] D. Metcalf, S. Nickell and R. Richardson, 'The structure of hours and earnings in British manufacturing industry', *Oxford Economic Papers*, vol. 28 (new series), 1976.

Hood and Rees[1] except that they used data for 1960–3. Following them, we argue that the number of days lost is an indicator of union strength in an industry, while taking the point that in some cases unions may gain concessions without the need to resort to stoppages. NCA, the proportion of adult male workers not subject to a collective agreement on pay and conditions in 1973, is also used as an inverse measure of union power. While this measure too may be criticised, we take the view that it provides a useful alternative to days lost as a means of measuring the effect of union power on inter-industry wage differences.

Table 6.5. *Regressions of hourly earnings on concentration and other variables across 49 industries, 1970*

	Equation number[a]		
	(1)	(2)	(3)
Concentration ratio	0.0078	0.0139[b]	0.0181[b]
	(0.0060)	(0.0061)	(0.0068)
Trade union (TUA)		0.0023[b]	
		(0.0006)	
Trade union (NCA)			−0.0248
			(0.0133)
Skill		0.0298[b]	0.0316[b]
		(0.0106)	(0.0119)
Region		0.0043	0.0121
		(0.0069)	(0.0073)
$\bar{R}^2$	0.014	0.411	0.265

SOURCES: See appendix 6A.
[a] Standard errors in brackets.
[b] Significantly different from zero at 5 per cent level.

Table 6.5 sets out the results. Taken on its own, concentration has a positive but non-significant effect. But after the introduction of the trade union variables and when allowance has been made for variations in skill and regional variations across industries, concentration becomes significant. We interpret this to mean that allowing for skill differences (the regional variable is non-significant) hourly earnings are higher in more concentrated industries, an effect which is obscured if these variables are not allowed for. The second column in table 6.5 predicts that an industry with 1 percentage point higher concentration adds about £1.40 a year, or 0.14 per cent to basic earnings (assuming a basic 40 hour week, 50 week year). We can evaluate the effect of a rise in concentration from 10 per cent to 60

[1] W. Hood and R. D. Rees, 'Inter-industry wage levels in United Kingdom manufacturing', *Manchester School of Economic and Social Studies*, vol. 42, 1974.

per cent when setting the values of the other variables equal to their means. Such a rise increases hourly earnings in the United Kingdom by 7 per cent, which contrasts with the larger effects identified by Phlips, who found that a rise in $C4$ from 10 to 60 per cent was associated with an increase in wages of 16 per cent in Belgium, 27 per cent in France and 43 per cent in Italy.[1] While there is some positive effect of concentration on hourly earnings in the United Kingdom therefore, it does not appear to be dramatic.

It should be borne in mind, however, that whilst from the point of view of the total wage bill the positive effect of concentration on employee compensation may be small, from the point of view of monopoly profit it is much larger. Although average employee compensation in the sample of industries selected is about the same as average Census of Production gross profit, it is much larger than average profit as normally defined because accounting profits are normally calculated after the deduction of selling, transport and some other costs which have to be included in the Census of Production definition. Moreover, only a part of average accounting profit may be attributed to monopoly. Hence a 7 per cent increase in the total wage bill is equivalent to a much larger percentage increase in monopoly profit. Thus the amount of monopoly rent is likely to be underestimated if attention is confined to profits and if no allowance is made for the absorption of part of monopoly rent by wages and salaries.

EFFICIENCY AND INDUSTRIAL CONCENTRATION

The evidence summarised in the previous sections suggests that oligopoly rents are small. Moreover, parts of them are absorbed by wages. It is possible that potential rents are absorbed in general slack or inefficiency; that is, that the leading firms in highly concentrated industries are content with their secure market positions and simply opt for a quiet life, instead of continually striving to increase their efficiency in order to increase their market shares. If this is the case we should expect the highly concentrated industries to be less efficient, in both the static and dynamic senses, than the more competitive industries. Thus we have to measure the static and the dynamic efficiency of British industries.

Static efficiency

Perhaps the commonest measure of the average technical efficiency of an industry at one point in time is labour productivity. This measure is very much a third best solution to the problem of measuring static efficiency. Its shortcomings are well known, but some of them can be overcome by using

[1] L. Phlips, *Effects of Industrial Concentration: A Cross Section Analysis for the Common Market*, Amsterdam, North-Holland, 1971.

comparisons of the labour productivity of the same industry in different countries. Such comparisons remove the problems of trying to compare physical output *per capita* in different industries in one country. On the other hand, problems raised by industries having different capital–labour ratios in different countries may still remain, even in the developed economies of Canada, France, West Germany, Sweden, the United Kingdom and the United States.

There are many variables which influence labour productivity, but in the first instance they may be grouped into 'country effects' and 'industry effects', excluding of course the different concentration ratios in each industry which are specified separately. For example, the different ratios of labour to capital in different industries would be included in 'industry effects' and the different factor ratios in the same industry in different countries would be included in 'country effects'. Table 6.6 arrays data on

Table 6.6. *Labour productivity (LP), concentration and size of plant in eight industries in five countries relative to the United States*

Indices, US = 100

	Beer brewing	Cigarettes	Paints	Crude petrol	Shoes	Glass bottles	Cement	Steel
UK								
LP	33	30	23	74	62	47	63	46
C_3	46	147	154	279	68	83	135	100
Plant size	30	24	78	134	60	47	88	43
Canada								
LP	73	61	56	125	95	..	107	95
C_3	133	135	123	215	64	..	142	180
Plant size	33	15	58	39	49	..	120	75
Sweden								
LP	27	75	49	137	73	85	96	54
C_3	87	152	146	294	105	154	154	87
Plant size	6	8	60	47	20	48	119	19
France								
LP	54	85	31	90	78	56	82	66
C_3	36	152	54	235	45	71	126	100
Plant size	18	9	29	111	66	74	114	47
W. Germany								
LP	42	51	33	64	..	..	82	76
C_3	10	141	100	212	..	..	72	100
Plant size	13	12	47	64	..	..	110	73

SOURCE: F. M. Scherer, A. Beckenstein, E. Kauffer and R. D. Murphy, *The Economics of Multi-Plant Operation – An International Comparisons Study*, Harvard University Press, 1975, tables 3.9, 3.12 and A 3.7.

physical output *per capita* in eight industries in five countries, expressed as percentages of the corresponding labour productivity in the United States. For example, labour productivity in the cigarette industry in the United Kingdom is only 30 per cent of labour productivity in the United States cigarette industry. Here concentration is the market share of the three top firms in each industry. This particular example is consistent with the hypothesis that high concentration is associated with low labour productivity. Indeed there are interviews to support the belief that the relatively low labour productivity in the British cigarette industry may be attributed in part to the relatively low intensity of competition.

Our interviews provided considerable qualitative evidence that pure X-inefficiency was a significant cause of productivity differentials. A tour through a European cigarette plant, for example, revealed that the machines were essentially the same as those used in other countries, but that 'traditional' machine manning standards were much looser. Executives in several British industries admitted that productivity had hovered at low levels because cartel arrangements fostered complacent attitudes. Sharp improvements were achieved in two cases after competition emerged following cartel dissolutions induced by the Restrictive Trade Practices Act.[1]

However, the relationship between productivity and concentration is more complicated than is suggested by this quotation. In the cigarette industries in France and Sweden there is an even higher degree of concentration than in the British cigarette industry, yet labour productivity is higher. Indeed if the simple regression of labour productivity on concentration is calculated from the data in table 6.6, a significant *positive* relationship of 0.221 (± 0.059) emerges, with $\bar{R}^2 = 0.262$, and this appears to be inconsistent with the belief that a greater degree of oligopoly makes for more inefficiency. But this simple regression is also misleading because it does not allow for the 'industry' and 'country' effects. When these are specified in a regression model with dummy variables as in table 6.7, it can be seen that concentration ratios or degrees of oligopoly have no negative effect on labour productivity; variations in this efficiency measure are also explained by the other variables subsumed under the industry and country dummy variables.

Thus the evidence does not support the hypothesis that high concentration breeds inefficiency. It is true that the United Kingdom tends to have lower labour productivity than the other countries investigated, but this tendency is not explained by variations in industrial concentration. Of course, the data relate to only eight industries and there is no reason to suppose that they are representative of all industries. Also, it

[1] Scherer *et al.*, *The Economics of Multi-Plant Operation*, pp. 74–5; 'X-inefficiency' is equivalent to our term 'slack'.

Table 6.7. *Regressions of labour productivity on concentration and size of plant across 37 industries, with industry and country dummy variables*

	Equation number[a]			
	(1)	(2)	(3)	(4)
Constant	39.27	34.73	20.91	36.64
Concentration	0.221[b]	0.191[b]	0.208[b]	0.213[b]
	(0.059)	(0.063)	(0.055)	(0.099)
Plant size		0.151		
		(0.112)		
Canada			37.01[b]	
			(10.49)	
Sweden			22.90[b]	
			(10.17)	
France			25.52[b]	
			(10.19)	
Germany			15.05	
			(10.97)	
Cigarettes				−7.17
				(13.93)
Paints				−22.79
				(12.43)
Petrol				8.81
				(21.41)
Shoes				26.95[b]
				(11.67)
Glass bottles				−4.80
				(13.15)
Cement				22.60
				(12.89)
Steel				6.63
				(12.34)
$\bar{R}^2$	0.262	0.279	0.424	0.492

SOURCE: Table 6.6.
[a] Standard errors in brackets.
[b] Significantly different from zero at 5 per cent level.

is extremely difficult to compile comparable physical measures of efficiency for the same industry in different countries and, although Scherer and his colleagues made every effort to overcome the formidable measurement problems involved, it is still possible that their estimates of physical productivity are not strictly comparable. For example, they indicate themselves that the figure for labour productivity in the United Kingdom brewing industry is too low because of the inclusion of transport workers excluded by other countries. Nevertheless, the fact remains that their pioneer study contains most of the limited economic knowledge available on variations in physical productivity between different industries in different countries and it clearly indicates that there is no association between concentration and labour productivity when the relationship is properly specified. Thus, provided that these eight industries are typical, we must conclude that there is no tendency for more concentrated industries to be less efficient than more competitive industries, although the conclusion must be provisional until the required data are available for a larger number of industries, so that we have more than the 37 observations used in table 6.7.

Dynamic efficiency

The above comparison of static technical efficiency and concentration is interesting but it is not sufficient, for in the long run 'it is dynamic performance that counts', to use the words of Scherer on the relationship between market structure and technological innovation. Scherer's summary of the extensive American literature on this relationship concludes that there is a threshold effect of the size of firm on dynamic efficiency: 'a little bit of bigness – up to sales levels of roughly $75 million to $200 million in most industries – is good for invention and innovation. But beyond the threshold further bigness adds little or nothing, and it carries the danger of diminishing the effectiveness of inventive and innovative performance.'[1] His survey of the relationship between concentration and innovation reaches the same conclusion.

Schumpeter was right in asserting that perfect competition has no title to being established as the model of dynamic efficiency. But his less cautious disciples are wrong when they imply that powerful monopolies and tightly-knit cartels have any stronger claim to that title. What is needed for rapid technical progress is a subtle blend of competition and monopoly, with more emphasis in general on the former than the latter, with the role of monopolistic elements diminishing when rich technological opportunities exist.[2]

The conclusion by Scherer on the threshold effect of size of firm on innovation was attributed to Markham.[3] In a subsequent survey of market concentration and innovation, Markham concludes that 'innovational effort is not spread throughout American industry in neat proportion to the concentration indexes for those industries. In fact such effort appears to increase with concentration only up to a certain threshold level, and much of it seems to be centered in a relatively small number of oligopolistic

---

[1] Scherer, *Industrial Market Structure and Economic Performance*.
[2] *Ibid*. pp. 377–8.
[3] J. W. Markham, 'Market structure, business conduct and innovation', *American Economic Review*, vol. 55 (Papers and Proceedings), 1965.

industries where technological opportunities are unusually large.'[1] In the discussion following his survey, Markham states clearly that the positive correlation between concentration and technological innovation does not specify the direction of causation – which must be borne in mind when interpreting table 6.8, which shows current expenditure by companies on research and development (R & D) as a percentage of net output and of turnover in seventeen manufacturing industries or groups of industries in 1968. Here capital expenditure is excluded, as is all government-funded R & D expenditure, which amounted to nearly 32 per cent of total R & D expenditure in 1968. Also excluded are the R & D expenditures in 'metal manufacture', because of steel nationalisation, and in 'other manufacture', because of the excessive heterogeneity of this residual category.

The use of R & D expenditure to measure the propensity to invent and innovate is traditional, as is the objection that such expenditure reflects inputs rather than the 'output' of technological innovation. But there is no satisfactory measure of the 'output' of such innovations in different industries. However, the ranking of industries in the first column of table 6.8 may be used to array the industries in order of importance as technological innovators, on the reasonable assumption that there is a high correlation between R & D inputs and outputs. The second column provides an alternative measure of R & D input with turnover as the denominator instead of net output. The ranking is broadly similar except for petroleum products, which have a small net output in relation to the cost of the raw materials used. Because of this, it is better to take net output as the denominator when measuring research effort, rather than turnover which includes the cost of raw materials.

The concentration ratios in table 6.8 are taken from chapter 2, although it was necessary to use employment-weighted averages of C_5 in those cases where R & D expenditure was given for groups of MLH industries. A comparison of the first and third columns shows that industries with high (low) R & D expenditure tend to have high (low) concentration ratios. A scatter diagram brings out the positive correlation, although there is no indication of a non-linear relationship and thus there is no evidence to support the argument that above a certain threshold level of C_5 there is no tendency for R & D expenditure to increase. Nevertheless the evidence of table 6.8 is not conclusive since rich technological opportunities exist for research in the industries with relative high R & D expenditure. The fact that, for example, the level of R & D expenditure in aerospace is more than eight times that in textiles, clothing, leather and footwear in relation to their respective net outputs cannot be attributed primarily to the higher

[1] J. W. Markham, 'Concentration: a stimulus or retardant to innovation' in H. J. Goldschmid, H. M. Mann and J. F. Watson (eds.), *Industrial Concentration: the New Learning*, Boston, Little, Brown and Co., 1974.

Table 6.8. *Research and development expenditure and concentration, United Kingdom 1968*

Percentages

	R & D as proportion of:		Concentration ratio
	Net output	Turnover	
Electronics and telecommunications	11.29	6.66	68
Petroleum products	10.28	1.27	88
Industrial engines	8.16	4.26	88
Aerospace	6.86	3.81	72
Pharmaceutical and toilet preparations	6.27	3.78	39
Electrical machinery	4.99	2.90	57
Plastics	4.87	2.14	52
Other chemicals	4.24	1.78	65
Instrument engineering	3.84	2.43	37
Motor vehicles	3.75	1.48	63
Machine tools	3.14	1.98	32
Other electrical engineering	2.88	1.34	55
Other mechanical engineering	1.86	1.03	31
Food, drink, tobacco	0.96	0.27	57
Textiles, clothing, leather, footwear	0.77	0.34	31
Metal goods, n.e.s.	0.74	0.35	25
Shipbuilding, marine engineering	0.51	0.31	52

SOURCES: Department of Trade and Industry, 'Resources devoted to research and development by manufacturing industry', *Economic Trends*, March 1974; chapter 2.

level of concentration in aerospace; it is simply because the general body of scientific knowledge provides more scope for research in aerospace than in textiles. Because it is not possible to distinguish between the separate effects of concentration and technological opportunities for research there is no point in presenting a formal regression analysis.[1] But this does not prevent us from concluding that there is no evidence that high concentration is associated with dynamic inefficiency: if anything, highly concentrated industries tend to be leading spenders on R & D, although this may be due to their technological and scientific base rather than to their oligopolistic nature.[2]

CONCLUSIONS

The survey of the evidence on profit-margins and oligopoly showed that there is no general tendency for margins to increase with increases in the

[1] With more observations, including a breakdown of R & D expenditure by MLHs, it would be worthwhile to perform a formal multiple regression analysis using a dummy variable to measure 'technological opportunities for research'.

[2] This suggestion is consistent with Freeman's summary of the relationship between innovation and the size of firm: he stresses that the major source of variations in research intensity between firms is the industry concerned (C. Freeman, *The Economics of Industrial Innovation*, London, Penguin, 1974).

degree of industrial concentration. This is not surprising. The difference between receipts and costs is obviously dependent on a very large number of economic and non-economic forces: the stochastic part of profit must be very large and we should not expect the traditional microeconomic theories of oligopolistic competition, which predict higher profit-margins in the more concentrated industries, to include all the variables which determine profits. In some industries the standard theory is relevant and provides valuable insights into the policies of some oligopolists. But it cannot be generalised to all oligopolists.

For government industrial policy, the implication is that the existing case-by-case approach of the Monopolies and Mergers Commission should continue. There is no justification for a blanket condemnation of highly concentrated industries on the grounds of profiteering. Equally, there is no justification for the view of some industrialists that the way to increase profitability is to increase industrial concentration.

Of the many other systematic forces which may influence profit-margins, two were surveyed in this chapter: labour costs and efficiency. There is some evidence that labour absorbs part of the potential oligopoly rents which arise in the standard theoretical models. It is known that the variation of wage changes across industries is very low, because of the tendency for differentials to be maintained, and it is not surprising that a large increase in concentration, from 10 to 60 percentage points, produces only a 7 per cent increase in wages. The suggestion[1] that there should be further study of the problems involved in referring restrictive labour practices to the Monopolies and Mergers Commission is to be welcomed. But there should also be further study of the effects of industrial concentration on wages and salaries.

Finally, the evidence surveyed on efficiency provided no grounds for claiming that an increasing degree of monopoly tends to reduce efficiency. It may be that examples can be found, such as the higher concentration of the British tobacco industry producing lower efficiency than in Germany or in the United States. But these examples cannot be generalised. Even in the tobacco industry, there is no association between concentration and labour productivity when the number of countries compared is increased to include Canada, France and Sweden. Once more, the case-by-case investigation explaining the low efficiency of some British industries is the correct approach to adopt. Policies designed to increase or decrease industrial concentration are unlikely to have a significant effect on average efficiency. The causes of our relatively low efficiency are too complicated.

The evidence presented in this chapter is statistical and necessarily excludes important forces which cannot be measured. The *threat* of import

---

[1] *A Review of Monopolies and Mergers Policy*, Cmnd 7198, p. 43.

competition may be important enough to prevent high prices or profit-margins in some industries but it cannot be measured by observed import statistics. Again, the possibility of an investigation by the Monopolies and Mergers Commission, the Office of Fair Trading, or the Price Commission may also prevent highly concentrated industries from profiteering. The effect of trade unions on wages can be measured but the constraints imposed upon oligopolists by trade union power are more difficult to assess. It seems likely, however, that they would press for higher wages if high profits were earned and, because of this, there may be limited gains for an oligopolist pursuing high profits unless he bargains with a weak trade union. It may be better for him to use his market power to minimise the variation in profitability over time and earn satisfactory rather than maximum profits.

This does not mean that an oligopolist can opt for a quiet life. There is always the danger that a 'thruster' from another industry will compete by producing substitutes or making a takeover bid. Such potential competition is another constraint on the pricing policy of an oligopoly. There are so many checks and balances in the real world which do not feature in standard theoretical models of imperfect competition that it is not surprising that observed market performance varies so little with actual market structure. For some industries the checks and balances may not operate and prices, profits or wages may be high, or efficiency low, but these special cases are best investigated by the Monopolies and Mergers Commission in the traditional British case-by-case approach.

SUMMARY OF FINDINGS

THE GROWTH OF INDUSTRIAL CONCENTRATION

This book has reviewed the growth of industrial concentration in this country over the period 1935–75 and its causes and effects. Economists use the term 'oligopoly' to describe the case where a few large firms are responsible for most of the sales, output or employment of an individual industry. Thus this book is concerned with increases in the degree of oligopoly within industries rather than with the related problems raised by the evolution of giant firms and their diversification across many industries. Concentration ratios, defined as the proportion of an industry's employment or sales controlled by its five largest enterprises, are normally used to measure the degree of oligopoly. There are alternative measures, but even using the same measures, different investigators have reached different conclusions on the growth of industrial concentration, partly as the result of changing samples of industries, including some which were subsequently nationalised. In chapters 2 and 3 we assessed the results of other authors and provided alternative detailed and consistent measurements of changes in average industrial and product concentration based on large constant samples.

Although average industrial concentration has increased since 1935, the first year for which reliable measures are available, this increase has not taken the form of a steady upward drift. A slow rise in 1935–58 was followed by a considerable acceleration in the decade 1958–68; while the period after 1968 witnessed a sharp deceleration in the increase in concentration. The share of the three largest enterprises in the total employment of the typical manufacturing industry in 1935 was 26 per cent; it reached 29 per cent by 1951, 32 per cent by 1958 and then increased sharply to 41 per cent by 1968. But between 1968 and 1973 this average concentration measure probably rose by only 1 percentage point or so. This general upward trend contrasts sharply with that in the United States, where average concentration increased by only about 2 percentage points over the whole period 1947 to 1970. Over the corresponding postwar period the increase in average industrial concentration in the United Kingdom was much greater, of the order of 12 percentage points. Clearly, the recent deceleration in this increase in the United Kingdom, which will be welcomed by those who wish to encourage competition, is long overdue.

Behind these average trends lie a wide variety of changes in different industries. For example, sixteen industries in Order III (food, drink and tobacco) had a mean increase in concentration of 16.1 percentage points (from 39.6 to 55.7) over the five years 1958–63 — an outstanding increase which played an important part in the acceleration of the average increase in industrial concentration after 1958. At the other extreme there were falls in Order IV (coal and petroleum products) and Order XVII (timber and furniture).

An interesting conclusion of our analysis of the general trends in industrial concentration is that the relatively rapid increase between 1958 and 1968 was not due to the faster growth of industries which were more highly concentrated in 1958. This implies that being in a highly concentrated industry does not guarantee a faster than average growth rate. In fact, there has been no tendency since 1958 for oligopolists to increase their business at the expense of the more competitive industries. There is some evidence, however, that this tendency was more important before 1958 when the average increases in industrial concentration were small.

A second conclusion which emerges from the analysis is that there was no tendency for an increase in concentration in any one industry in the period 1958–63 to persist in the following period 1963–8. This implies that even during times of a very rapid increase in average industrial concentration, there is no tendency for such an increase in an individual industry to be continuous as the result of irresistible economic forces; on the contrary, an increase in one quinquennium gives no guide to the size of concentration change in the next.

If we measure concentration in more narrowly defined product groups as in chapter 3, on the grounds that this level is nearer to the concept of the market than is the typical Census of Production industry, then the share of the five largest enterprises in the total sales of the typical product grew from 55.4 per cent to 63.4 per cent between 1958 and 1968. But there is no reliable evidence to suggest that the rate of change in 1958–63 differed from that in 1963–8, notwithstanding the claims made by other authors that this was the case. Although the rate of increase in average product concentration was steady in the period 1958–68, there was a marked change after 1968. Between 1968 and 1975 the average product concentration ratio rose by less than 2 percentage points to 65.1 per cent. This clear deceleration in the increase in average concentration occurred in spite of higher merger activity in the early 1970s. This 'bend in the trend' may be a mere short-term pause, but it serves as a warning to those who believe that increases in industrial concentration are inevitable.

Product groups may be regarded as sub-divisions of industries in the Census of Production, but in practice many products of an industry are excluded when concentration ratios are calculated, mainly because their sales are relatively small or because a concentration ratio might disclose confidential information relating to an individual firm. Thus in practice industrial and product concentration ratios are not always good substitutes for each other. In these circumstances it is advisable to analyse the two levels of concentration separately. Fortunately, over the period studied, both analyses lead to the same general conclusions: a similarity in the average trend since 1958; the absence of persistent increases in concentration for individual products in the consecutive periods 1958–63 and 1963–8; and similar changes in the averages for Industrial Orders and product groups. For example an increase of 11.1 percentage points in mean concentration for the 28 products in Order III (food, drink and tobacco) in the period 1958–63 compared with 16.1 per cent for the Order as a whole. This broad consistency in results is comforting because the Census of Production does not contain sufficient information at product level to analyse the causes and effects of increases in product concentration. The consistency of our findings at product and industry levels justifies our use of the statistics available at industry level to investigate the causes and effects of increases in the degree of oligopoly.

THE CAUSES OF THE GROWTH OF INDUSTRIAL CONCENTRATION

The forces influencing industrial concentration are so complex and so numerous that many authors attribute most, if not all, of the increase in concentration to a multitude of small chance or stochastic effects. We have considerable sympathy with such views, but we believe that some systematic factors, such as plant economies of scale and mergers, have effects which are large enough to be separately identified and measured.

Chapter 4 specified three systematic variables thought to be important determinants of the *level* of industrial concentration; plant economies of scale, industry size and the ratio of the number of plants to enterprises in an industry. The regressions justified this specification, particularly when the logarithms of variables were used. However, when changes in the logarithms of these systematic factors and in industrial concentration were considered for the decade 1958–68 it became clear that other variables had to be included; only 17 per cent of the variation in concentration change between industries was explained. The additional variables considered were the initial concentration level in 1958, expenditure on advertising, and mergers.

The logarithm of the initial concentration level had an important effect in the regression analysis, but we regard this effect as primarily statistical although economic effects may play a minor role. But advertising expenditure, which many authors claim has a tendency to increase industrial concentration, had no significant effect. Moreover, it continued to be insignificant when the regressions were modified to allow for separate effects in consumers' and producers' goods industries. Many tests were performed besides those reported in this book, but none revealed that advertising had any effect on changes in industrial concentration.

But perhaps expenditure on mergers is the most interesting variable from the point of view of government policy. Unfortunately, information on mergers is only available at the Industrial Order (two-digit) and not at the MLH (three-digit) level. However, we were able to include the effect of mergers in the regression analysis by using the variable for expenditure on mergers in each Order to measure the importance of mergers in each industry within that Order. In fact, this measure of mergers does have a significant effect on industrial concentration although its addition explains only a further 4.6 per cent of the variation of the logarithmic changes in concentration between industries. Nevertheless, its effect is as important as the average of the three systematic variables considered at the outset.

It must be emphasised that the analysis of variance in appendix 4B which yields these results is concerned with variation between industries and clearly demonstrates that the differential internal growth rates of firms, reflected by the variance of the residuals, is important. If the inter-industry variation is ignored, and if our attention is focused on the contribution of each systematic factor to the change in concentration of the average industry, then the importance of mergers and of other systematic factors would be considerably increased because, by definition, the mean of the residuals in the regression equation, measuring the average stochastic effect, must be zero. Because of this, and because of other problems explained in appendix 4B, we cannot perform a statistical decomposition of the mean change in concentration; we have to analyse the variance, even though the variance of mergers expenditure is underestimated because of lack of data at the industry level.

To overcome the limitations of the available statistics on mergers, we have used case studies to obtain a better assessment of the importance of mergers in increasing concentration. Regression analysis is clearly insufficient by itself to enable us to identify the major causes of the growth of industrial concentration. Case studies at the level of the census product (four-digit) are summarised in chapter 5. At this level concentration ratios were found to be increased by forward integration and by government policy in the form of the Restrictive Trade Practices Act and the IRC, in addition to being increased by mergers. Low entry barriers, high initial concentration levels, limitations on the acquisition of enterprises, and market growth made for decreases in concentration.

Chapter 5 also showed that in 1958–68 mergers were primarily responsible for increases in concentration in fourteen products out of a sample of 27. Moreover, the average increase in concentration in these fourteen products was 15.4 percentage points, compared with the 7.8 percentage points in the six products which had concentration increases without mergers. The remaining seven products had decreases in concentration. Clearly, the case studies suggest that mergers were responsible for a substantial proportion of the increases in concentration over the decade 1958–68, possibly half. Although it is impossible to estimate this proportion with any precision using case studies, it is obvious that the statistical estimate of 4.6 per cent based on the analysis of variance is too low: the estimate based on the case studies is preferable. This does not imply that the stochastic factors influencing increases in concentration were negligible. On the contrary these were also very important. Moreover in the period since 1968, when merger expenditure continued to be substantial, there has been very little increase in product or industry concentration. It is true that conglomerate mergers, which are unlikely to affect product or even industry concentration ratios, became more important after 1970. But horizontal mergers were still preponderant and the absence of any substantial increase in average concentration since then emphasises the relevance of all the stochastic factors responsible for the differential internal growth of firms.

To find out more about the determinants of industrial and product concentration, we need more case studies to reveal the different forces at work in each case. Such descriptive studies will also reveal the dynamics of the changes in concentration, including the composition and rank order of the five largest firms, which are hidden by the Census of Production concentration ratios.

THE EFFECTS OF THE GROWTH OF INDUSTRIAL CONCENTRATION

One reason why the governments of many western countries have policies to control monopolies in the private sector is the fear that they tend to create unnecessarily high prices, low outputs, and high profits. As the degree of oligopoly increases these detriments may also increase. The effects of monopoly, oligopoly and the like on price increases is associated with the so-called 'administered price' hypothesis and may be a partial explanation of the phenomenon of stagflation, the coincidence of rising prices and falling output.

The evidence presented in chapter 6 showed that increases in concentration over the period 1963–8 had no significant effect on price increases. The main determinants of the variation of price increases between industries were variations in costs, as measured by labour productivity and raw-material prices. Increases in wages were associated with the average increase in prices, but the variation of wage increases between industries was sometimes too small to produce a significant regression coefficient. This extremely low dispersion of wage increases between industries, together with the high dispersion of productivity increases, is consistent with the 'key industry' explanation of the wage-spiral, although it does not necessarily follow that the industries which led the upward pressure for wage increases were the same over time.

We have also assessed the relationship between changes in price–cost margins and changes in concentration. When comparable industries are selected there is no relationship between the change in concentration and the change in the price–cost margin. Various time lags were introduced but they did not affect this basic result. Perhaps we should not be very surprised at this. The stochastic part of profit must be very large, if only because profit, however defined, is a residual. We should not expect standard microeconomic theories of imperfect competition to include all the variables which influence profitability. For some industries such theories may help us to understand and analyse the behaviour of oligopolists; for other industries they may not be very helpful. If we use census data to measure profitability, the evidence provides no justification for the belief that in general highly concentrated industries tend to be more profitable. This result justifies the traditional case-by-case approach of the British Monopolies and Mergers Commission.

However, census data are inadequate. The numerator of net output less employee compensation is only a crude measure of profit. In particular it includes depreciation and it might be argued that this tends to be large in oligopolies because their access to cheap sources of finance leads to excessive capital expenditure. They also pay higher wages. Oligopolies could therefore have excessively high prices offset by excessively high costs and still have price–cost margins, as defined in the census, which look reasonable. One way to assess such a possibility is to compare the costs, especially wages, of the highly concentrated industries and the rest. This was also done in chapter 6. The effect of concentration on hourly earnings was found to be positive but small. If wage costs are higher in oligopolies, and if they offset excessive capital expenditure to leave price–cost margins much the same as in the more competitive industries, then the excess capital expenditure cannot be very great. Nevertheless, the fact that labour absorbs part of the potential excess profit of oligopolies has obvious relevance for any government policy on prices and incomes.

An alternative explanation of the absence of any strong correlation between price–cost margins and concentration is that oligopolies tend to be less efficient than firms in more competitive industries and this slack offsets their higher prices. No case could be established for this assertion from a review of the evidence; there may be oligopolists who tolerate excessive slack and opt for a quiet life, but there are proportionately as many cases of this in the less concentrated industries. If an oligopolist opts for a quiet life, there is a danger that a 'thruster' from elsewhere will market a substitute product or make a successful takeover bid.

The popular view is that private industry is being increasingly concentrated under the control of fewer and fewer firms as the result of technological economies of scale; furthermore that this process results in higher prices, higher profit-margins and possibly higher money wages; also that it fosters economic and technical inefficiency. There is a grain of truth in these popular views, but only a grain. The increase in business concentration is continuous, but not at a steady rate. Nor is it persistent. Moreover, although systematic forces explain a significant part of the increase, a substantial part is due to stochastic factors influencing the differential internal growth of firms.

Stochastic models, which represent an important advance over simple deterministic models, have been used extensively in summarising the complex patterns of the growth of firms. A recent National Institute study[1] explains such models and it is unnecessary to repeat the mathematical arguments here. Suffice it to say that in the simplest stochastic model firms in an industry are like particles in a cloud of gas. They have a wide disparity of size, with large numbers of small particles and a few large particles, and their sizes are changing all the time as the result of random multiplicative shocks which are independent of size. Thus the chance of a large particle growing, or declining, by 10 per cent is the same as that for a small particle. In more complex stochastic models the chance of a 10 per cent growth depends on previous growth, or on current size. Moreover, some particles are combining, some are transferring unwanted parts to other particles. The net result of all this activity is that the disparity of the sizes of particles increases over time; the total share of the cloud occupied by the largest particles increases and this holds even though the total size of the cloud increases over time. In addition, the rank order of particles changes; the largest particle in one year is not the same as in another year. The cloud is dynamic, not static.

In the context of firms, these models would stress the dynamic nature of industries. Consumers' tastes are always changing; new products are being marketed; overseas markets are affected by wars, famines, droughts, and revolutions; competitive goods are being imported. All this makes it difficult for firms to fulfil their plans; mistakes are made, excess capacity arises in some parts of industry while order-books lengthen in other parts,

---

[1] Prais, *Evolution of Giant Firms*.

giving a superficial appearance of inefficiency. It is not surprising that firms try to minimise the amount and the speed of adjustment to these changes, by trying to reduce the intensity of competition with a view to minimising the fluctuations in profits rather than to earn excess levels of profit. Nor is it surprising that in such a world the effect of the degree of concentration on price changes, price–cost margins, wages and efficiency is either small or insignificant: too many other forces are at work.

THE NEXT STEPS

These conclusions do not mean that government intervention through institutions such as the Monopolies and Mergers Commission is unnecessary. On the contrary, such institutions form part of the forces which constrain the entrepreneurial behaviour predicted by various theoretical models of the firm; if a firm seeks high profits without attracting the attention of a government agency, it would be well advised to ensure that its profit-margin is not excessive. Government agencies clearly have an important role as referees to prevent the violation of the rules of the competitive game. To perform this function adequately, they need up-to-date information on concentration and market performance. At the moment Census of Production data are several years out of date and it seems extremely difficult to reduce this time lag. One step which could be taken to speed up publication would be to relax the disclosure rules so that it would no longer be necessary to spend a great deal of time ensuring that concentration data did not reveal information relating to an individual firm. A second valuable step would be the publication of more detailed product (five-digit) concentration ratios. These would identify the products to be monitored for excessive prices, price-leadership and other violations of the competitive rules.

Assuming that better data become available, what should be the next steps in research into concentration? One important project would involve measuring the persistence of concentration changes. This would highlight those industries or products with persistent increases in concentration, in addition to showing the average value of the serial correlation of concentration changes. Secondly, the deceleration of the upward trend in concentration after 1968 needs closer examination when the data for more recent years become available. Thirdly, the relationship between technical efficiency and concentration requires more extensive investigation; the number of industries studied in the international comparisons in chapter 6 is small and the sample may be unrepresentative. Such an extension also requires more data, which are difficult to compile, but it would certainly be worth doing.

Above all we need more case studies, especially of industries and products where concentration is very high. Such studies may be unfashionable, but they are essential to improving our understanding of the dynamics of concentration. The data may be difficult to compile, but the very act of compilation involves studying company reports, reading trade journals, visiting firms, talking to businessmen and civil servants, and all of these activities guarantee that the complexity of the economy is burned into the soul of the research worker.

THE MEASURE OF CONCENTRATION

As explained in the Preface, there is no need to review the advantages and disadvantages of the concentration ratio compared with all the other measures of concentration. However, it is worth summarising the reasons why we prefer the concentration ratio to the Hirschman–Herfindahl H-index, which is simply the sum of the squared values of the share of each enterprise in the total employment (or sales etc.) of the industry concerned. It is also worth explaining why we have made no attempt to correct the concentration ratios for imports.

The H-index can be derived from standard models of neoclassical microeconomic theory. This is an advantage, but the weight attached to it depends on the value of the particular theoretical model in analysing imperfect competition in the real world and we give a small weight to this. It certainly does not outweigh the disadvantages of using the H-index. The first is that official estimates of the H-index, unlike the concentration ratio, are not available for the period studied. Unofficial estimates have to be derived from the size distributions of enterprises published in the Census of Production and critical assumptions have to be made about the dispersion of enterprises within each size class, especially in the largest size class which is usually open-ended. The value of these unofficial estimates is heavily dependent on the particular assumptions made and thus measurement errors may be serious, whereas the official concentration ratios are calculated from the original, confidential, ungrouped data and are exact. Secondly, the H-index is based on the whole size distribution whereas the concentration ratio relates to the upper tail. Thus the H-index is more sensitive to the different number of firms in each industry and because of this it may be a misleading guide to the degree of competition. If the five top enterprises lead an industry's price and output policies, it does not matter whether ten or fifty enterprises follow this lead. The disadvantage of the H-index, even if calculated from ungrouped data, is that in many cases the difference between values of H in different industries is due to differences in the number of enterprises which are unlikely to reflect corresponding differences in the degree of competition. The fact that *on average* H is more sensitive than C_5 to a change in N may be demonstrated by comparing the relevant elasticities. Using data on H, C_5 and N for 75 industries in Hart and Morgan[1] and in appendix 2C it was found that the regression coefficient of $\log H$ on $\log N$ was -0.569 (0.058) compared with -0.387 (0.043) for the regression of $\log C_5$ on $\log N$. Thirdly, Theil has shown that the decomposition properties of H make it an undesirable measure of the effects of mergers on concentration.[2]

Thus there are good reasons for preferring the concentration ratio to the H-index. Nevertheless, it must be stressed that neither is more than a preliminary screening device to indicate industries where competition is likely to be more or less intensive. Detailed case studies, or even investigations by the Monopolies and Mergers Commission, are needed to ascertain whether the high degree of monopoly indicated by a high level of C_5 or H for a particular industry is misleading or not. On average, industries with low values of C_5 or H are likely to be more competitive than those with high values, but this average tendency might not hold for a particular industry. Again, a strong tendency for average C_5 or H to increase over time indicates that the intensity of competition within industries is decreasing *on average*, although there are no doubt examples of particular industries with increased C_5 or H where the intensity of competition has not diminished.

Note that the term 'degree of monopoly' has been used in the popular, or even legal, sense of being the opposite to the intensive rivalry of competition. Saving[3] shows that an increase in the weighted average C_5 does not necessarily imply an increase in the average value of either the Lerner or the Rothschild 'degrees of monopoly', which are simply transformations of price-elasticities derived from neoclassical economic theory. Although an increase in the weighted average C_5 from 20 per cent to 90 per cent over one year does not necessarily imply that the Lerner or Rothschild measures increase at all, it does not follow that there is no change in the intensity of competition, defined in terms of rivalry rather than in terms of price-elasticities. This distinction between the different definitions of the degree of monopoly is important: in this book we have tried to avoid using the term 'degree of monopoly' and we have referred to 'intensity of competition', or even 'degree of oligopoly', in order to distinguish our approach from that of Lerner or of Rothschild.

Both the concentration ratio and the H-index are usually derived from domestic data and it could be argued that in practice imports constitute such an important constraint on the activities of the domestic producers that some attempt should be made to include imports in the measure of concentration used. For example, we could add imports to the total sales in

[1] Hart and Morgan, 'Market structure and economic performance'.
[2] H. Theil, *Statistical Decomposition Analysis*, Amsterdam, North-Holland, 1972, p. 43.
[3] T. R. Saving, 'Concentration ratios and the degree of monopoly', *International Economic Review*, vol. 11, 1970.

the denominator of a domestic concentration ratio and the resulting decrease in the concentration measure would reflect greater intensity of competition. However, there are good reasons for not making such corrections. First, the data on the ratio of imports to sales are not generally available below the MLH (three-digit) level of aggregation, and it is likely that many imports recorded at this level are inputs into domestic production in the same industry and thus complementary to rather than competitive with domestic sales. Secondly, in a world of multinational enterprise, it is likely that even those imports which are competitive are in part controlled by the largest domestic firms and thus correction of concentration measures for imports would be misleading. Thirdly, the *threat* of competitive imports would also constrain the actions of the largest domestic firms and we are unable to measure this import potential. For these reasons, the correction of concentration ratios for imports is likely to be uncertain in its effects and may introduce variations between industries which do more harm than good. Hence in this study no attempt has been made to correct concentration ratios for imports. This is not to say that such corrections may not be desirable, but they would require more information than is at present available in published government statistics.

APPENDIX 2A

WEIGHTED MEAN CONCENTRATION RATIOS

In a sample of m industries the weighted mean concentration ratio is given by

$$\bar{C}_w = \sum_{j=1}^{m} W_j C_j \Big/ \sum_{j=1}^{m} W_j \qquad (2\,\text{A.}1)$$

where W_j denotes the weight to be attached to the concentration ratio for the jth industry ($j = 1, 2, \ldots, m$). If W_j is the same for each industry, say W, then the equally weighted mean results:

$$\bar{C} = W \sum_{j=1}^{m} C_j \Big/ mW = \sum_{j=1}^{m} C_j \Big/ m \qquad (2\,\text{A.}2)$$

and the relationship between them is given by

$$\bar{C}_w - \bar{C} = \rho_{cw} \sigma_c \eta_w \qquad (2\,\text{A.}3)$$

where ρ_{cw} is the correlation between C_j and W_j across the m industries, σ_c is the standard deviation of C_j, and η_w is the coefficient of variation of W_j.[1] Clearly, since $\sigma_c \geqslant 0$ and $\eta_w \geqslant 0$ the sign of $\bar{C}_w - \bar{C}$ is the sign of ρ_{cw}. Thus if the employment-weighted mean is smaller than the equally weighted mean concentration ratio there is a negative correlation between the size of industry measured by its employment and its level of concentration.

In the present context of employment concentration ratios the ratio C_j has its weight W_j as its denominator. Suppose the jth industry has n enterprises, then the five-enterprise concentration ratio is

$$C_5 = \sum_{i=1}^{5} W_{ij} \Big/ \sum_{i=1}^{n} W_{ij} \qquad (2\,\text{A.}4)$$

where W_i is the employment of the ith enterprise, with W_1 denoting the employment of the largest enterprise, and where

$$\sum_{i=1}^{n} W_{ij} = W_j \qquad (2\,\text{A.}5)$$

[1] For example, see G. U. Yule and M. G. Kendall, *An Introduction to the Theory of Statistics*, London, Griffin, 1957, pp. 332–4.

denotes the total employment in the jth industry. Thus the employment-weighted mean concentration ratio is

$$
\begin{aligned}
\bar{C}_w &= \sum_{j=1}^{m} W_j \left(\sum_{i=1}^{5} W_{ij} \middle/ W_j \right) \middle/ \sum_{j=1}^{m} W_j \\
&= \sum_{j=1}^{m} \sum_{i=1}^{5} W_{ij} \middle/ \sum_{j=1}^{m} W_j
\end{aligned}
\left. \right\} \qquad \text{(2 A.6)}
$$

and the denominator of $\bar{C}_w$ is the total employment in all the m industries. It is known that the distribution of W_j across all industries is approximately log-normal with large positive skewness so that the change in $\bar{C}_w$ will be heavily influenced by changes in the concentration ratios of a few large industries.[1] Since these changes may not be typical, there is a case for preferring the equally weighted mean, $\bar{C}$.

The decomposition of the total change in the current-weighted mean into the effects of the mean change in concentration and the effects of changes in weights is most easily formulated by putting $a = W/\Sigma W$ to give

$$
\begin{aligned}
\bar{C}_{wt} - \bar{C}_{w0} &= \Sigma a_0 C_{5t} - \Sigma a_0 C_{50} + \Sigma a_t C_{5t} - \Sigma a_0 C_{5t} \\
&= \Sigma a_0 (C_{5t} - C_{50}) + \Sigma C_{5t}(a_t - a_0)
\end{aligned}
\left. \right\} \quad \text{(2 A.7)}
$$

when the weights on the change in concentration are those at time 0. When weights at time t are used, we have

$$
\begin{aligned}
\bar{C}_{wt} - \bar{C}_{w0} &= \Sigma a_t C_{5t} - \Sigma a_t C_{50} + \Sigma a_t C_{50} - \Sigma a_0 C_{50} \\
&= \Sigma a_t (C_{5t} - C_{50}) + \Sigma C_{50}(a_t - a_0)
\end{aligned}
\left. \right\} \quad \text{(2 A.8)}
$$

Equations (2 A.7) and (2 A.8) are used in the analysis of the change in mean concentration ratios (current weights) in tables 2.1 to 2.6 and tables 3.1, 3.2 and 3.4.

The effect of changes in weights may be seen by rewriting (2 A.3) as

$$
\bar{C}_w - \bar{C} = \text{Cov}(C,W)/\bar{W} \qquad \text{(2 A.9)}
$$

where $\bar{C}_w$ denotes the mean concentration ratio with current-year weights and $\bar{W}$ denotes the mean of those weights. With time subscripts 0 and t, we have

$$
(\bar{W}_t/\bar{W}_0)\,[(\bar{C}_w - \bar{C})_t/(\bar{C}_w - \bar{C})_0] = \text{Cov}(C,W)_t/\text{Cov}(C,W)_0 \quad \text{(2 A.10)}
$$

which is used to compile tables 2.10 and 3.5.

---

[1] See Aitchison and Brown, *The Lognormal Distribution*; P. E. Hart and E. H. Phelps Brown, 'The sizes of trade unions: a study in the laws of aggregation', *Economic Journal*, vol. 67, 1957.

THE SELECTION OF COMPARABLE INDUSTRIES

1935–51

The 98 industries in table 2.1 are those left after four exclusion procedures were applied to the 185 trades and sub-trades identified by Evely and Little as having 'a prima facie basis of comparability'.[1] The exclusion procedures were as follows:

(i) One trade, tin, was omitted since the largest producer in 1935 was not ranked amongst the three largest business units because of its small labour force.

(ii) Fifty-four trades and sub-trades were omitted because they were deemed non-comparable. Evely and Little's degree of comparability test was used here, an arbitrary acceptable level being set at 1 ± 0.1.[2]

(iii) Fourteen trades were omitted when information on a part of them was available, in order to avoid the duplication of data.

(iv) Finally, eighteen trades and sub-trades were omitted because concentration ratios for more than three business units were given for 1951 in these cases.

The major discrepancy between our exclusion procedures and those used by Evely and Little in deriving their sample of 41 trades and sub-trades[3] is that we have not eliminated trades whose estimated principal product concentration ratio ranges overlapped for the two years. As explained in the text, the application of this procedure may make the sample unrepresentative for the purpose of estimating average concentration trends, as well as significantly reducing the sample size. It must be noted that our results for the 98 trades may be less meaningful, however, because of the omission of this exclusion procedure.

1951–8

The 57 industries in table 2.2 are the 63 used by Armstrong and Silberston,[4] less seven for which the 1951 concentration ratio relates to

---

[1] Evely and Little, *Concentration in British Industry*, appendix J.

[2] The degree of comparability of each trade and sub-trade can be found in Evely and Little's appendix J. It is 'the ratio between the 1935 sales of principal products by establishments in the Census trade (and sub-trade) according to the 1948 Census and the same data for 1935 according to the 1935 Census' (*ibid*. p. 145).

[3] *Ibid*. chapter X.

[4] Armstrong and Silberston, 'Size of plant, size of enterprise and concentration'.

more than the three largest enterprises (margarine; dyestuffs; explosives; steel tubes; cutlery; leather goods; cement), plus one mining industry (metalliferous mining and quarrying). The 1951 concentration ratios were adjusted in order to include small firms.

1958–63

The 1958 Census identified 126 industries in manufacturing and mining, compared with 124 in the 1963 Census. The discrepancy is due to the amalgamation of coal tar products and general chemicals in the 1963 Census, and to the exclusion of textile converting from the 1963 Census. Of the 124 industries in the 1963 Census four were eliminated in addition to general chemicals: coal mining (because it was nationalised); mineral oil refining (because the 1958 data are not available at the five-enterprise level for disclosure reasons[1]); locomotives and railway track equipment, and railway carriages, wagons and trams (because of the large public sector in these industries). The remaining 119 industries are comparable, apart from possible minor changes between the two Censuses, and accounted for 97 per cent of all enterprise employment in manufacturing and mining in 1963 (excluding coal mining).

Sawyer used a comparable sample of 117 manufacturing industries for this period, omitting the four mining industries included here. He also omitted locomotives and railway track equipment; and railway carriages, wagons and trams because of the large change in the relative size of the private and public sectors.[2] He included both general chemicals and mineral oil refining, which are excluded from table 2.3.

1963–8

There are 149 industries in manufacturing and mining identified in the 1968 Census. Table 42A in part 158 of the 1968 Census gives information on them for 1963 and 1968. Twelve were eliminated as follows: coal mining was omitted as before; and five industries were omitted because of steel nationalisation, namely, metalliferous mining and quarrying, coke ovens, iron and steel (general), steel tubes, and iron castings. In addition locomotives, etc. and railway carriages, etc. were excluded as before, and a search through the industry reports revealed four industries in which 1963 and 1968 data were not comparable, namely, bacon curing, meat and fish products; milk and milk products; starch and miscellaneous foods; and industrial (including process) plant and steelwork. These four industries are noted in table 42A of the Census as non-comparable. A fifth

[1] They are available at the three-firm level however from Summary Table 5 in part 133 of the 1958 Census.
[2] Sawyer, 'Concentration in British manufacturing industry', p. 354. For locomotives, etc. private manufacturers employed 35 per cent of the industry's workforce in 1958 and 23 per cent in 1963. The figures for railway carriages, etc. are 74 per cent and 43 per cent respectively.

industry, petroleum and natural gas, etc., also thus noted in table 42A, has not been excluded. Other industries had minor incomparabilities, particularly as regards the treatment of small establishments, but these were judged to be insufficient to justify exclusion. One case, furniture and upholstery, was dubious however. This experienced a sharp fall in concentration in 1963–8, which may have been caused by a failure to exclude all production of seats for cars and aeroplanes from the 1963 data in accordance with the changed 1968 industry definition. The 137 industries remaining accounted for 89 per cent of employment in manufacturing and mining (excluding coal mining) in 1968.

1958–68

For the whole period 1958–68 the comparable sample of industries is much smaller because of the increased number of industries identified in the 1968 Census which was caused by breaking up and/or rearranging many former industries, particularly in the chemicals and engineering Orders. In selecting the 79 comparable industries the first step was to exclude any industry already excluded in either of the two sub-periods. The comparability of the remaining industries was then assessed by comparing total employment in 1963 according to Summary Table 1 in the 1963 and in the 1968 Censuses. In addition, changes in industry definitions were examined in the individual industry reports and the calculated concentration ratios 1963 (I) and 1963 (II) were compared (see appendix 2C). Industries were regarded as comparable 1958–68 if the estimates of 1963 employment in both Censuses were similar, with similar concentration ratios, and if they appeared to have had no change in definition according to the individual industry reports.

1970–3

The 132 industries of table 2.6 were selected from the 151 industries in manufacturing and mining in 1970 in Summary Table 9, part C154 of the 1970 Census of Production, as follows:

   (i) The eight industries with large public sectors as listed under 1963–8 above were omitted. Locomotives, etc. and railway carriages were treated as one industry in the 1970 Census.

   (ii) In addition, eleven 1970 industries were omitted because of changes in definition in 1973 compared with 1970; in most cases this was due to the industries being split into two or more in the later years. The industries involved were: petroleum and natural gas, salt and miscellaneous non-metalliferous mining (MLHs 104, 109 (3) (4)); refrigerating machinery (339 (3)); space heating and air-conditioning equipment (339 (4)); food and drink processing machinery (339 (7)); miscellaneous (non-electrical) machinery (339 (5) (6) (8) (9)); general mechanical engineering (349);

broadcast receiving and sound reproducing equipment (365); miscellaneous electrical goods (369); motor vehicle manufacturing (381); hosiery and other knitted goods (417); and bricks, fireclay and refractory goods (461).

(iii) Finally, ordnance and small arms (MLH 342) was omitted due to non-disclosure of information.

In 29 of the remaining 132 industries it was necessary to estimate the employment C_5 by the methods described in appendix 2C. The concentration ratio was estimated for eleven industries in 1970 and nineteen industries in 1973, there being one industry (tobacco (MLH 240)) for which C_5 was estimated in both years. The 132 industry sample represented 79 per cent of employment in United Kingdom manufacturing and mining (excluding coal mines) in 1973. The 1973 concentration data were taken from Summary Table 13 of the 1973 Census of Production.

Whilst we can be reasonably confident about the comparability of the 132 industries over the period 1970–3, it should be noted that new census practices introduced in the annual Censuses of Production from 1970 may have introduced additional imprecision to census data. In the context of concentration data, the most important point would seem to be the new census practice of estimating the left-hand tail of the firm size distribution. In contrast to the five-yearly censuses, where small establishments were required to report the nature of their work done and the average number of persons they employed, in the annual censuses establishments with less than 25 employees (in some cases less than 11) or whose employment is not known are not required to make a census return. Moreover, in the interests of reducing the lag before publication it appears that the residual category 'unsatisfactory returns' is now taking a more prominent position in the reported census results.

As an illustration of the size of these problems, it is reported in the 1970 Census that forms were sent to 51,000 establishments compared with an estimated 88,000 establishments in all manufacturing.[1] Moreover, by August–September 1971 the authorities reported 18,000 non-respondents. Presumably some proportion of such non-respondents remained at the time of preparation of the Summary Table results, and it is not clear that all such establishments were necessarily smaller establishments. Be that as it may, it is clear that in terms of numbers of establishments (but, of course, much less so in terms of proportion of activity)[2] a great deal of estimation

---

[1] *Report on the Census of Production 1970*, part C1, p. 6. See also part C154, Summary Table 1.

[2] Nevertheless, estimates for non-returns and small establishments in terms of activity appear not to be negligible. Thus, for example, 1972 provisional results were published in late 1973 with coverage of an estimated 71 per cent of employment, a figure which was substantially lower for some industries. Estimated coverage for the final results must be higher than this, of course, but by how much is not reported.

of figures was involved in the reported census results. It is just not known how accurate such estimation is, but it seems clear that some additional arbitrariness must be involved in these procedures. This factor must also be borne in mind when considering concentration trends, particularly over the short period 1970–3 considered in chapter 2. Since estimates must be based on extraneous, presumably past, data, it may be that this imparts some spurious stability to concentration estimates over short periods in some broad sense. As far as individual industry concentration is concerned, one suspects that year-on-year comparisons since 1970 may well have little meaning with respect to many industries.

ESTIMATING CONCENTRATION AT THE INDUSTRY LEVEL, 1958–68

The industry concentration ratios for 1958, 1963 and 1968 have been estimated graphically from size distributions of enterprises in the Census of Production.[1] These tables were employed to construct cumulative concentration curves on semi-logarithmic graph paper, the cumulative number of enterprises being plotted on the logarithmic scale against cumulative percentages of total employment. Such curves were drawn by hand through the points down to the three largest enterprise level. Three- and five-enterprise concentration ratios for each industry and each year were then read from the freehand curve. Where appropriate, separate estimates for 1963 were made corresponding to the two 1963 data sources which differ because of changes in definition. Concentration ratios were estimated to the nearest integer. Care was taken to ensure that the curves passed within the maximum and minimum possible three- and five-enterprise concentration ratios consistent with the available data.

Suppose the distribution of enterprises by employment for an industry has m size classes, with frequencies n_i and aggregate employments of y_i $(i = 1, 2, \ldots, m)$ in each class, with subscript 1 denoting the largest size class. Thus the employment concentration ratio based on the largest n_1 enterprises is simply $y_1/\Sigma_{i=1}^{m} (y_i)$ and is given by the size distribution. If it is desired to estimate C_r and if $r > n_1$, then a minimum estimate may be obtained by assuming that all the n_2 enterprises in the second largest class have the same employment, y_2/n_2, and adding $(r-n_1)y_2/n_2$ to y_1 to obtain

$$\min C_r = [y_1 + (r-n_1)y_2/n_2]/\Sigma y_i \qquad (2\,\text{C}.1)$$

Similarly the maximum concentration ratio is estimated by assuming that the $r-n_1$ have the upper limit of employment in class 2, subject to the constraint that the remaining $n_2 - (r-n_1)$ enterprises in this class cannot have less than the lower limit of employment. That is,

$$\max C_r = [y_1 + (r-n_1)y_a]/\Sigma y_i \qquad (2\,\text{C}.2)$$

---

[1] Data for 1958 and 1963 are available in table 3 of the individual industry reports for those years, whilst data for 1963 (again) and 1968 are available in Summary Table 42A of the 1968 Census, part 158, pp. 14–115. In addition, employment concentration ratios for five or more enterprises for 1958 are available in Summary Table 5 of the 1958 Census, part 133, pp. 96–105. Data from table 3 of the industry reports were supplemented by estimates of employment in all firms (including unsatisfactory returns) given in Summary Table 1 of the 1963 Census, part 131, pp. 10–27.

where y_a is the upper limit of class 2. If this estimate implies that the residual $n_1 + n_2 - r$ enterprises in class 2 have employment below y_b, the lower limit of class 2, then

$$\max C_r = [y_1 + y_2 - (n_1 + n_2 - r)y_b]/\Sigma y_i \qquad (2 \text{ C}.3)$$

If $r < n_1$, then

$$\min C_r = (r.y_1/n_1)/\Sigma y_i \qquad (2 \text{ C}.4)$$

and

$$\max C_r = [y_1 - (n_1 - r)y_a]/\Sigma y_i \qquad (2 \text{ C}.5)$$

where y_a is the lower limit of the largest class.

In many cases the range of possible outcomes is narrow so that the margin for error of the graphical estimates is small. Where, however, the range is large, and this particularly applies to cases where $r < n_1$, it is possible that significant measurement errors arise. In such cases it might be argued that it would be better to use the average of the maximum and minimum possible ratios, the procedure adopted by Sawyer. But this procedure is arbitrary and the results obtained are highly sensitive to the amount of data available for calculating the ranges. One of several examples of this is the watches and clocks industry. For 1958 the possible range of $C4$ estimated by Sawyer was 70.7 to 71.2 per cent, so that an estimate of 71 per cent is subject to little error. For 1963 (I), however, the possible range is much wider: 54.1 to 77.1 per cent, implying a five points fall in concentration in the period 1958–63.[1] However, our curves show that concentration increased in this industry in this period and suggest that the true $C4$ was about 76 or 77 per cent. Moreover, it is known from the published size distributions that at the six-enterprise level concentration was six points higher in 1963. In fact we know from data in the 1968 Census, which were not available to Sawyer, that $C4$ was 76 per cent in 1963 in this industry. The graphical approach, by presenting a clear picture of the industry, reduces the likely error attached to estimates of concentration and this may be demonstrated by other examples.

The accuracy of our $C5$ estimates for the year 1968 has been checked more directly using a special tabulation of five-enterprise concentration ratios kindly made available to us by the BSO. This tabulation provides five-enterprise employment concentration ratios at the MLH level. In contrast to our estimates, however, unsatisfactory returns are omitted from the denominator of the concentration ratio, so that we would expect the ratios on average to be slightly higher than our own. Our *a priori* expectations are borne out by a scatter diagram which was drawn for 146

---

[1] Sawyer, 'Concentration in British manufacturing industry'; based on 1963 census data.

of the 149 MLH industries in manufacturing and mining in 1968.[1] The scatter was homoscedastic, and the ordinary least-squares regression (with standard errors in brackets) was:

$$C_5(A) = 0.955 + 0.999\ C_5(B) \qquad R^2 = 0.9964$$
$$\quad\ (0.274)\ \ (0.005) \qquad\qquad n = 146$$

As expected the BSO ratios are larger on average than our estimates, and this is confirmed by a comparison of unweighted mean ratios: the mean of $C_5(B)$ being 49.4 compared to 48.4 for $C_5(A)$. The goodness of fit and slope of unity for the regression line, however, provide us with strong support for the graphical method of estimating C_5.

Thus we are reasonably confident that our estimates of C_5 for 1968, and by implication for the earlier years also, do not err markedly or systematically from the true concentration ratios. Table 2C.1 gives estimates of C_5 for the years 1958–68 obtained by the graphical method; estimates are given for MLH industries as defined in 1968 wherever possible, although only for the 79 industries in italics are the ratios comparable for the whole period 1958–68. Concentration estimates for 1958 and 1963(I) are provided in table 2C.2 for ten industries which were radically redefined in 1968.

Table 2C.1. *Estimated five-enterprise employment concentration ratios by Orders and MLHs, 1958, 1963 and 1968*

Percentages

Order	MLH		1958	1963 I	1963 II	1968
II	102	*Stone, slate quarrying*	19	22	22	25
	103	*Chalk, clay, sand, gravel*	24	33	35	42
	109(1,2)	Metalliferous mining	70	75	75	97
	104 109(3,4) }	*Petrol, gas, other mining*	78	82	82	70
III	211	*Grain milling*	49	56	56	61
	212	*Bread and flour confectionery*	24	60	60	66
	213	*Biscuits*	50	61	61	70
	214	Bacon curing, meat, fish	28	38	38	35
	215	Milk products	39	51	47	34
	216	*Sugar*	94	96	96	98
	217	*Cocoa, chocolate, sugar confectionery*	41	54	54	59
	218	*Fruit and vegetables*	37	41	42	49
	219	Animal and poultry foods	26	39	43	44
	221	Oils and fats	65	59	53	46

[1] In addition to coal mining, two further mining industries (metalliferous mining and quarrying; and petroleum and natural gas, salt, etc.) were excluded from the comparison because the BSO uses different definitions of these industries from those used in Summary Table 42A of the 1968 Census of Production. Also, for purposes of comparison with our estimates, the BSO data (which were to one decimal place) were rounded to the nearest whole number.

Table 2C.1. (continued)

Percentages

Order	MLH		1958	1963 I	1963 II	1968
	229(1)	*Margarine*	84	89	89	95
	229(2)	Starch and miscellaneous	31	34	34	32
	231	*Brewing and malting*	22	50	49	61
	232	Soft drinks	..	..	45	47
	239(1)	*Spirit distilling*	82	79	79	71
	239(2)	British wines, cider and perry	..	..	78	80
	240	*Tobacco*	90	97	97	98
IV	261	Coke ovens, etc.	65	63	63	91
	262	Mineral oil refining	..	94	94	88
	263	*Lubricating oils, greases*	38	40	39	44
V	271(1)	General chemicals (inorganic)	..	..	70	61
	271(2)	General chemicals (organic)	..	..	69	67
	271(3)	General chemicals (other)	..	..	59	48
	272	Pharmaceuticals	34	32	39	39
	273	*Toilet preparations*	35	32	32	40
	274	Paint	..	..	38	33
	278	Fertilizers	..	..	79	85
	279(1)	*Polishes*	56	63	63	65
	279(2)	Adhesives, gelatine, etc.	50	65	61	51
	279(3)	Explosives, fireworks, etc.	92	88	85	85
	279(4)	Pesticides, disinfectants	..	..	43	52
	279(5)	Printing ink	..	..	57	62
	279(6)	Surgical bandages, etc.	..	..	78	79
	279(7)	Photographic chemicals	..	..	93	89
	275	*Soap, detergents*	67	75	75	69
	276	Synthetic resins, etc.	61	66	55	52
	277	Dyestuffs, pigments	..	..	75	75
VI	311	Iron and steel (general)	40	47	47	73
	312	Steel tubes	82	77	77	81
	313	Iron castings, etc.	21	27	27	35
	321	Aluminium and alloys	..	..	51	44
	322	Copper, brass, etc.	..	..	50	56
	323	Other base metals	..	..	49	50
VII	331	Agricultural machinery	47	43	36	40
	332	*Machine tools*	25	27	26	32
	333	Pumps, valves, compressors	..	..	23	27
	334	Industrial engines	60	71	65	88
	335	Textiles machinery	45	49	46	46
	336	Construction equipment	39	38	32	34
	337	Mechanical handling plant	28	26	22	26
	338	*Office machinery*	49	61	61	54
	339(1)	Mining machinery	..	..	37	47
	339(2)	Printing, etc. machinery	..	..	48	51
	339(3)	Refrigerating machinery	..	..	74	64
	339(4)	Space-heating machinery	..	..	29	24
	339(7)	Food and drink equipment	..	..	38	43
	339(5,6,8,9)	Other machinery	12	12	24	23
	341	Industrial plant	23	24	23	20

Table 2C.1. (continued)

Percentages

Order	MLH		1958	1963 I	1963 II	1968
	342	Ordnance and small arms	81	74	77	80
	349	General mechanical engineering	18	17	22	29
VIII	351	Photographic equipment	..	..	57	78
	352	*Watches and clocks*	73	78	78	81
	353	Surgical appliances	..	..	23	23
	354	Scientific instruments	..	..	22	33
IX	361	*Electrical machinery*	51	52	53	57
	362	*Insulated wires, cables*	67	73	73	82
	363	*Telegraph and telephones*	80	84	86	92
	364	Radio components	..	..	44	44
	365	Broadcast equipment	..	..	66	72
	366	Electronic computers	..	..	92	88
	367	Radio, radar and electronic goods	..	..	69	66
	368	Electric appliances (domestic)	50	49	44	48
	369	*Miscellaneous electrical goods*	40	40	40	47
X	370	*Shipbuilding*	40	43	43	52
XI	380	Wheeled tractors	..	..	91	93
	381	*Motor vehicles*	46	54	52	60
	382	*Motor cycles, etc.*	67	73	73	83
	383	*Aerospace equipment*	61	68	68	72
	384	Locomotives	72	76	88	96
	385	Railway carriages, etc.	54	62	88	92
XII	390	*Engineers' small tools*	16	16	16	17
	391	*Hand tools, implements*	20	29	29	35
	392	Cutlery, spoons, forks, etc.	38	52	41	35
	393	Bolts, nuts, screws etc.	38	48	43	45
	394	*Wire, wire manufactures*	28	32	32	34
	395	*Cans, metal boxes*	70	72	72	75
	396	Jewellery, precious metals	24	30	33	46
	399(1)	Metal furniture	..	..	31	27
	399(5)	Drop forgings, etc.	..	..	50	52
	399(6,7)	Metal hollow-ware	..	..	25	28
	399(10,11)	Other metal goods	..	..	9	11
XIII	411	*Man-made fibres*	91	99	99	100
	412	*Spinning and doubling*	28	32	32	43
	413	*Weaving of cotton, linen*	10	15	14	29
	414	*Woollen and worsted*	12	18	18	21
	415	*Jute*	49	60	60	62
	416	*Rope, twine and net*	40	51	51	57
	417	*Hosiery, etc.*	12	18	18	30
	418	*Lace*	20	28	28	21
	419	*Carpets*	39	35	35	42
	421	*Narrow fabrics*	22	25	25	30
	422(1)	*Household textiles*	10	14	14	20
	422(2)	*Canvas goods and sacks*	14	17	17	15
	423	*Textile finishing*	27	28	28	37
	429(1)	*Asbestos manufactures*	74	79	79	81

Table 2C.1. (continued)

Percentages

Order	MLH		1958	1963 I	1963 II	1968
	429(2)	*Miscellaneous textiles*	23	34	36	42
XIV	431	*Leather (tanning and dressing)*	13	14	14	18
	432	*Leather goods*	11	14	13	15
	433	*Fur*	14	23	23	20
XV	441	*Weatherproof outerwear*	16	23	23	28
	442	*Men's, boys' outerwear*	27	32	32	34
	443	Women's, girls' outerwear	12	16	13	13
	444	*Overalls, men's shirts, etc.*	11	15	15	22
	445	*Dresses, lingerie*	5	9	10	16
	446	*Hats, caps, millinery*	17	22	22	28
	449(1,3,4)	*Corsets and miscellaneous*	18	21	21	36
	449(2)	*Gloves*	22	29	29	32
	450	*Footwear*	17	19	20	23
XVI	461	*Bricks, fireclay etc.*	24	27	27	40
	462	*Pottery*	17	20	20	41
	463	*Glass*	53	52	52	58
	464	*Cement*	88	90	90	95
	469(1)	*Abrasives*	69	73	73	81
	469(2)	*Other building materials*	20	20	19	20
XVII	471	*Timber*	7	7	7	11
	472	*Furniture, upholstery*	17	16	16	8
	473	*Bedding, soft furnishings*	22	25	26	29
	474	*Shop, office fittings*	15	12	12	9
	475	*Wooden containers, baskets*	8	9	9	10
	479	*Wooden and cork manufactures*	7	9	9	11
XVIII	481	*Paper and board*	39	42	42	43
	482(1)	*Cardboard boxes, etc.*	29	33	33	35
	482(2)	Other paper packaging products	..	..	41	37
	483	Manufactured stationery	..	..	40	38
	484	Other paper and board	23	27	38	41
	485/6	*Newspapers and periodicals*	34	48	48	47
	489	*General printing, etc.*	8	10	10	12
XIX	491	*Rubber*	40	44	43	47
	492	*Linoleum, plastic floorings*	80	62	62	65
	493	*Brushes, brooms*	24	32	32	39
	494	Toys, games, etc.	38	41	36	46
	495	*Stationers' goods*	33	34	34	33
	496	*Plastics products*	16	13	13	14
	499	Other manufacturing	34	36	17	17

SOURCES: Censuses of Production.

Notes: (i) 1963 I from 1963 Census; 1963 II from 1968 Census.
(ii) Items in italics have concentration ratios comparable for the whole period.

Table 2C.2. *Estimated five-enterprise employment concentration ratios of ten industries,*
1958 and 1963[a]

Percentages

Order	MLH		1958	1963
III	239(2,3)	Soft drinks, wines, etc.	27	44
IV	271(1)	Dyestuffs	91	92
	271(2)	Fertilizers and pesticides	64	65
	271(3)	General chemicals	45	48
	274	Paint, printing ink	26	32
V	321/2	Non-ferrous metals	31	30
VI	351	Scientific, surgical, photographic	23	25
	364	Radio, electronic apparatus	31	40
VIII	389	Prams, hand-trucks, etc.	38	45
IX	399	Other metal manufactures	8	10

SOURCE: 1963 Census of Production.
[a] Based on the 1958 Standard Industrial Classification: see text.

THE CLASSIFICATION OF INDUSTRIAL
CONCENTRATION BY INDUSTRIAL ORDER

The samples of industries used in chapter 2 to estimate changes in mean industrial concentration were not random: they were the largest possible samples of comparable industries for each time period. This appendix presents a series of tables which show the extent to which the samples are representative of all orders in the SIC in each period. This classification also highlights the sectors of British industry where the largest increases in concentration have taken place.

1951–8

The limited sample of 57 industries in table 2.2 allows a partial classification of concentration trends in the period 1951–8 by broad industry group. Thirty-eight of the industries are classified in six SIC (1968) Orders in table 2D.1. The remaining nineteen industries were scattered across nine other Industrial Orders in which too few industries were classified to be representative. Only one of the six Orders in table 2D.1 (coal and petroleum products) experienced a fall in average

Table 2D.1. *Concentration changes in six 1968 Industrial Orders, 1951–8*

		Coverage		Concentration ($\bar{C}_3$)		
Order		1958 employment	No. of industries	1951	1958	Change 1951–8
		(%)		(percentages)		
III	Food, drink, tobacco	82	10	33	38	+5
IV	Coal and petroleum products	100	3	59	56	−3
V	Chemicals	39	8	41	42	+1
XIII	Textiles	54	10	26	29	+3
XVIII	Paper, printing, etc.	87	4	18	21	+3
XIX	Other manufacturing	55	3	34	36	+2

SOURCES: See appendix 2B.

concentration over the period. Of the three industries in this Order, two had decreases while one was unchanged. The other five Orders had rises in mean concentration. The textile Order was notable in that eight of the ten industries in our sample increased in concentration (five industries from this Order were omitted from the sample). More striking, however, was food, drink and tobacco, in which nine out of ten of the industries sampled had concentration increases (again, five industries were omitted). This finding is interesting in that, as we shall see, this sector also experienced by far the largest increase in mean concentration in the period 1958–63.

1958–63

The 119 comparable industries in table 2.3 are classified by Industrial Order (1968) in table 2D.2. Only two Orders show a fall in concentration, measured by the 1958 employment-weighted mean, and both of these falls are small. Timber, furniture, etc., had a fall of 0.2 percentage points, although three of the six industries in this Order increased in concentration. Coal and petroleum had a concentration fall of 0.9 percentage points; of the two industries in this group, coke ovens decreased in concentration by 2 percentage points, and lubricating oils and greases

Table 2D.2. *Distribution of 119 industries by 1968 SIC Orders, with mean* C_5 *1958–63*

		Coverage		Weighted mean $C_5{}^a$		
Order		1963 employment	No. of industries	1958	1963	Change 1958–63
		(%)		(percentages)		
II	Mining and quarrying[b]	100	4	35.9	41.3	5.4
III	Food, drink and tobacco	100	16	39.6	55.7	16.1
IV	Coal and petroleum products[c]	56	2	57.3	56.4	−0.9
V	Chemicals[d]	64	10	54.2	56.3	2.1
VI	Metal manufacture	100	4	38.2	42.1	3.9
VII	Mechanical engineering	100	11	27.1	27.9	0.8
VIII	Instrument engineering	100	2	27.5	29.7	2.2
IX	Electrical engineering	100	6	48.4	51.9	3.5
X	Shipbuilding	100	1	40.0	43.0	3.0
XI	Vehicles[e]	90	4	53.3	60.8	7.5
XII	Metal goods n.e.s.	100	8	18.2	21.7	3.5
XIII	Textiles	100	15	23.1	27.9	4.8
XIV	Leather and fur	100	3	12.5	15.4	2.9
XV	Clothing and footwear	100	9	16.0	20.0	4.0
XVI	Bricks, pottery, etc.	100	6	32.1	33.3	1.2
XVII	Timber, furniture, etc.	100	6	12.5	12.3	−0.2
XVIII	Paper, printing, etc.	100	5	22.8	28.2	5.4
XIX	Other manufacturing	100	7	36.4	37.6	1.2
	Total	97	119	32.6	37.7	5.1

SOURCES: See appendices 2B and 2C.
[a] Weighted by 1958 employment.
[b] Coal mines are excluded.
[c] Mineral oil refining is omitted.
[d] General chemicals are omitted.
[e] Locomotives, etc. and railway carriages, etc. are omitted.

increased in concentration by the same amount, the overall fall being due to the weighting. The industry excluded from this Order, mineral oil refining, decreased in concentration at the C_3 level, for which information is available. Clearly, there is no Order for which it is possible to say that there was a marked tendency for concentration to decrease in this period.

Rather, the typical Order experienced an increase in mean concentration. Twelve groups, ranging from mechanical engineering ($+0.8$ percentage points) to textiles ($+4.8$ percentage points), had a rise in concentration of less than the 1958 employment-weighted average increase of 5.1 percentage points. This leaves only four with an above-average increase in concentration. Order II (mining and quarrying) and Order XVIII (paper, printing and publishing) had rises of 5.4 percentage points and are not markedly differentiated from textiles. Vehicles, with an increase of 7.5 percentage points, stands out more. But it is Order III (food, drink and tobacco) which experienced the largest concentration rise in this period, with an increase of no less than 16.1 percentage points at the industry level. The large rise in concentration in this group in the period 1951–8 has been noted already. In 1958–63, fourteen of the sixteen industries in Order III experienced increases in C_5, with only two (vegetable and animal oils and fats, spirit distilling and compounding) having concentration falls. Eight industries had concentration rises in excess of 10 percentage points. Bread and flour confectionery had a rise of 36 percentage points, while brewing and malting had a rise of 28 percentage points. These two outstanding industries were followed by soft drinks, British wines, cider and perry (17 points); animal and poultry foods (13 points); cocoa, chocolate and sugar confectionery (13 points); milk and milk products (12 points); biscuits (11 points); and bacon curing, meat and fish products (10 points). The large and widespread increases in concentration in Order III were a major factor in the overall increase in concentration in this period.

1963–8

The sample of 137 comparable industries in table 2.4 is classified by SIC Order (1968) in table 2D.3. Four Orders had a concentration fall as measured by the 1963 employment-weighted means. Orders IV and XVII continued the decline observed in 1958–63. Coke ovens were omitted from Order IV because they experienced a large concentration increase as the result of steel nationalisation. In Order XVII the overall concentration fall was produced by decreases in only two of the six industries included (furniture and upholstery; shop and office fittings). It is interesting to note that Orders IV and XVII were respectively the most and least concentrated in 1968, as measured by 1963 employment-weighted means. The other two Orders with concentration decreases in

1963–8 were chemicals and allied industries, and metal manufacture. In the chemicals group six industries had increases in C_5, eight had decreases and three had no change. The slight fall in concentration in metal manufacture (from which the three ferrous industries were omitted because of nationalisation) was due to a fall in concentration in the aluminium industry.

Table 2D.3. *Distribution of 137 industries by 1968 SIC Orders, with mean* C_5 *1963–8*

Order		Coverage		Weighted mean C_5		
		1968 employment	No. of industries	1963	1968	Change 1963–8
		(%)		(percentages)		
II	Mining and quarrying[a]	92	3	35.4	38.2	2.8
III	Food, drink and tobacco[b]	76	14	58.1	63.5	5.4
IV	Coal and petroleum products[c]	58	2	78.6	75.6	−3.0
V	Chemicals	100	17	59.8	57.7	−2.1
VI	Metal manufacture[d]	24	3	50.2	49.6	−0.6
VII	Mechanical engineering[e]	84	16	33.2	37.1	3.9
VIII	Instrument engineering	100	4	27.0	35.8	8.8
IX	Electrical engineering	100	9	57.4	61.4	4.0
X	Shipbuilding	100	1	43.0	52.0	9.0
XI	Vehicles[f]	94	4	59.5	66.0	6.5
XII	Metal goods n.e.s.	100	11	24.2	26.2	2.0
XIII	Textiles	100	15	28.6	36.2	7.6
XIV	Leather and fur	100	3	15.2	17.3	2.1
XV	Clothing and footwear	100	9	20.0	24.3	4.3
XVI	Bricks, pottery, etc.	100	6	33.6	42.7	9.1
XVII	Timber, furniture, etc.	100	6	12.3	10.6	−1.7
XVIII	Paper, printing, etc.	100	7	29.5	30.4	0.9
XIX	Other manufacturing	100	7	33.3	36.4	3.1
	Total	89	137	39.7	43.8	4.1

SOURCES: See appendices 2B and 2C.
[a] Omitting coal mines and metalliferous mining and quarrying.
[b] Omitting bacon curing etc.; milk and milk products; and starch and miscellaneous foods.
[c] Coke ovens omitted.
[d] Iron and steel (general); steel tubes, and iron castings omitted.
[e] Industrial (including process) plant, and steelwork omitted.
[f] Omitting locomotives, etc. and railway carriages, etc.

In the other fourteen Orders industrial concentration increased as measured by the 1963 employment-weighted mean. These ranged from Order XVIII (paper, printing and publishing) with an increase of 0.9 percentage points to Order XVI (bricks, pottery, glass, etc.) with a rise of 9.1 percentage points. No single group had an outstanding concentration increase in 1963–8, as was the case with Order III (food, drink and tobacco) in 1958–63. In fact Order III had a concentration increase of 5.4

percentage points, which was only slightly above average for 1963–8. Five groups had faster rises than this. Vehicles continued the increase in concentration observed in 1958–63, with an increase of 6.5 percentage points. Textiles, with a rise of 7.6 percentage points, appear to have had an acceleration in the rate of concentration increase. This tendency seems even more notable in the three groups with the largest rises: instrument engineering; shipbuilding and marine engineering; and bricks, pottery, etc.

It should be noted that these results at the industry level do not conform exactly with those derived at the product level in chapter 3. In particular, Order II (mining and quarrying) and Orders VII and IX (mechanical and electrical engineering), which are distinguished as having notable concentration increases at the product level, do not show this in table 2D.3. This acts as a warning: these results are only indicative of the sectors of the economy where the tendency to increase concentration is *likely* to have been operative.

1958–68

Table 2D.4 distributes 68 of the 79 comparable industries in table 2.5 into their 1968 Industrial Orders. Eleven industries and six Orders have been omitted because the industries classified in these Orders were responsible for less than half of the employment in the Order and could not be regarded as representative. Table 2D.4 also shows the levels and changes in the 1958 employment-weighted mean in the twelve Orders included. The six Orders omitted tended to have small changes in concentration in the period. Coal and petroleum products experienced small falls in concentration in 1958–63 and 1963–8, while both chemicals and metal manufacture had small falls in the latter period. Mechanical engineering, instrument engineering and metal goods n.e.s. all experienced concentration rises in both periods, but none was substantial, except that in instrument engineering in 1963–8 (see table 2D.3).

Of the twelve Orders in table 2D.4, only one experienced falling concentration. This was the least concentrated Order XVII (timber, furniture, etc.). At the other end of the scale, despite only two thirds coverage, Order III (food, drink and tobacco) clearly stands out as the leading sector in the tendency to increased concentration 1958–68, although three quarters of the concentration rise in this Order came in 1958–63. Less spectacular rises occurred in the other ten Orders. Order XI (vehicles) with a rise of 12.8 points led the way, followed by Order XIII (textiles) and Order X (shipbuilding) with rises of 12.7 and 12.0 points respectively. Other substantial increases occurred in bricks, etc. (10.3 points), clothing (9.3 points), mining (8.2 points) and electrical engineering (8.2 points).

Table 2D.4. Distribution of 68 industries by 1968 SIC Orders, with mean C5 1958, 1963 and 1968

Order		Coverage		1958 employment-weighted mean					
		1968 employment	No. of industries	1958	1963(1)[a]	1968	Change 1958–63	Change 1963–8	Change 1958–68
		(%)[b]				(percentages)			
II	Mining and quarrying	91[b]	3	30.7	36.1	38.9	5.4	2.8	8.2
III	Food, drink and tobacco	67	10	42.2	60.2	66.3	18.0	6.1	24.1
IX	Electrical engineering	57	4	55.3	57.1	63.5	1.8	6.4	8.2
X	Shipbuilding	100	1	40.0	43.0	52.0	3.0	9.0	12.0
XI	Vehicles	90	3	53.5	60.9	66.3	7.4	5.4	12.8
XIII	Textiles	100	15	23.1	27.8	35.8	4.7	8.0	12.7
XIV	Leather and fur	100	3	12.5	15.4	17.3	2.9	1.9	4.8
XV	Clothing and footwear	89	8	16.5	20.5	25.8	4.0	5.3	9.3
XVI	Bricks, pottery, etc.	100	6	32.1	33.3	42.4	1.2	9.1	10.3
XVII	Timber, furniture, etc.	100	6	12.5	12.3	10.6	−0.2	−1.7	−1.9
XVIII	Paper, printing, etc.	85	4	23.0	28.3	29.4	5.3	1.1	6.4
XIX	Other manufacturing	80	5	36.4	37.3	39.9	0.9	2.6	3.5
	Total	83	68	33.6	39.3	44.8	5.7	5.5	11.2

SOURCES: See appendices 2B and 2C.
a 1963 census data.
b Excluding coal mines.

1970–3

The sample of 132 comparable industries in table 2.6 is classified by Industrial Order (1968) in table 2D.5. In the eighteen Orders distinguished, industry concentration increased on average in ten and fell in eight. None of the sectors distinguished earlier as having marked concentration increases (with the exception of mining and quarrying) appear to have had such an increase in the period 1970–3. In particular, we may note that food, drink and tobacco, which exhibited dramatic concentration rises in the 1950s and 1960s, showed only a moderate increase in 1970–3. Of the other four sectors in table 2D.4 with over a 10

Table 2D.5. *Distribution of 132 industries by 1968 SIC Orders, with mean C5 1970 and 1973*

		Coverage		Weighted mean C_5		
Order		1973 employment	No. of industries	1970	1973	Change 1970–3
		(%)		(percentages)		
II	Mining and quarrying	92[a]	2	32.9	41.9	9.0
III	Food, drink and tobacco	100	17	56.9	58.3	1.4
IV	Coal and petroleum products	69	2	72.2	71.6	−0.6
V	Chemicals	100	17	58.5	57.5	−1.0
VI	Metal manufacture	24	3	52.9	51.7	−1.2
VII	Mechanical engineering	60	11	34.3	33.7	−0.6
VIII	Instrument engineering	100	4	39.3	38.8	−0.5
IX	Electrical engineering	78	7	60.5	60.2	−0.3
X	Shipbuilding	100	1	53.0	52.0	−1.0
XI	Vehicles	33	3	76.8	74.5	−2.3
XII	Metal goods n.e.s	100	11	24.2	24.9	0.7
XIII	Textiles	77	14	41.4	43.5	2.1
XIV	Leather and fur	100	3	18.1	19.9	1.8
XV	Clothing and footwear	100	9	23.3	25.4	2.1
XVI	Bricks, pottery, etc.	83	5	42.5	43.2	0.7
XVII	Timber, furniture, etc.	100	6	10.9	13.5	2.6
XVIII	Paper, printing, etc.	100	8	29.3	29.4	0.1
XIX	Other manufacturing	100	9	35.6	35.7	0.1
	Total	79	132	42.0	42.4	0.4

SOURCES: See appendix 2B.
[a] Excluding coal mines.

percentage point concentration increase in 1958–68, shipbuilding and vehicles had small concentration falls on average in 1970–3, whilst textiles and bricks, pottery, etc. had small rises. Only mining and quarrying showed a dramatic concentration rise in the period 1970–3, arising from a 10 percentage point concentration rise in stone and slate quarrying and mining (MLH 102) and an 8 percentage point increase in chalk, clay,

sand and gravel extraction (MLH 103). The moderate concentration
levels in these industries, 34 per cent and 49 per cent respectively in 1973,
would seem to indicate that there is little danger of monopolisation in these
cases at the present time.

THE 1975 INDUSTRY CONCENTRATION DATA

As explained in chapter 1, the 1975 data on industry concentration became available too late for systematic analysis in this book. This appendix offers a preliminary inspection of these data, with the principal conclusion that no dramatic changes were observed in 1973–5; if anything, there was a slight fall in concentration over this two-year period.

Table 2E.1 presents equally weighted and employment-weighted mean C_5 for 99 comparable industries in 1970, 1973 and 1975. These industries were the 132 comparable industries used for the period 1970–3 in chapter 2 less (a) pumps, valves and compressors (MLH 333), which was split into three separate industries in 1975, and (b) 32 further industries for which C_5 was not given exactly in 1975 for disclosure reasons. Whilst for 1970–3 graphical estimates of C_5 (as described in appendix 2C) were used in such cases, time constraints prevented our doing this for 1975. The 99 industries represented nearly two thirds of the industries and 62 per cent of the employment in manufacturing and mining (excluding coal mines) in 1970.

Table 2E.1. *Equally weighted and employment-weighted mean C_5 for 99 comparable industries, 1970, 1973 and 1975*

Percentages

	1970	1973	1975	Change 1970–5		
				In mean	In weights	Total
Equal weights	46.7	47.7	47.4	0.7	—	0.7
Employment weights						
1970	42.9	43.5	43.0	0.1	−0.1	—[a]
1975	43.0	43.6	42.9	−0.1	0.1	—[a]

SOURCES: See text.
[a] At current weights.

Table 2E.1 reveals a rise in concentration of 0.7 of a percentage point over the five years 1970–5 using equally weighted means, but virtually no change in concentration in this period using 1970 or 1975 employment-weighted means. The table shows small concentration increases for the period 1970–3, which are, as one would expect, similar to those observed in

129

table 2.6. For the period 1973–5, however, small falls in average concentration are recorded in the 99 comparable industries, which, in the case of the employment-weighted means, more or less offset the concentration rise recorded in 1970–3. As stressed in chapter 2, the small concentration increases observed in 1970–3 may be attributable to sampling variation and similar comments also apply to table 2E.1. The results of this appendix reinforce our conclusion of chapter 2 that the 1970s saw a deceleration in the rate of concentration increase compared with the high rates of increase observed in the period 1958–68.

SOURCES AND METHODS,
CHAPTER 3

Census of Production sales concentration ratios for products

Summary Table 5 of the 1963 Census (vol. 131, pp. 98–114) lists 277 products and provides concentration information for 1958 and 1963, whilst Summary Table 44 of the 1968 Census (vol. 158, pp. 118–64) lists 340 products, with information for 1963 and 1968. The information relates to sales, and generally refers to the five largest enterprises (ranked by sales) producing a product. All the products are drawn from United Kingdom manufacturing and mining industries, Orders I I–X I X of the latest (1968) S I C. The figures for mining apply to Great Britain only. Sales figures relate to all domestic output of a product, regardless of the M L H in which particular establishments making that product are classified. In the 1963 Census the data given exclude *firms* with less than 25 employees, while the 1968 Census excludes *establishments* with less than 25 employees.

The products for which concentration ratios are available were a non-random sample from all the principal products identified in United Kingdom manufacturing and mining by the Census. The sampling procedure was as follows. First, before the Census was compiled, an initial selection was made from the headings listed in the current census questionnaires, in an attempt to form items into homogeneous products. When the census results were known, a few products had to be eliminated for disclosure reasons, in accordance with the Statistics of Trade Act, 1947. In addition, products with total sales of less than £10 million were eliminated, although three products escaped this net in each year: electrical ware of porcelain, etc., rubber footwear and musical instruments in 1963; and internal combustion reciprocating engines, sewing machines and cigarette machinery in 1968. These selection procedures left 277 products in 1963 accounting for 72 per cent of total sales of principal products in manufacturing and mining and 340 products in 1968 accounting for 76 per cent of such sales. These average estimates exclude smaller firms in 1963 and smaller establishments in 1968.

Table 5 of any of the individual industry reports of the 1963 or 1968 Census shows that most of the products listed are small with sales of less than £10 million. In many cases the BSO aggregated items into 'homogeneous products' and included them in the Census. By its very

131

nature this procedure is somewhat arbitrary but it seems to meet the economists' requirement of homogeneity, for heterogeneous items were not aggregated. For example, in the grain milling industry in 1968, there were three products (white flour for bread-making, other flour and cereal breakfast foods in packets for retail sale) accounting for 77 per cent of sales, and nineteen other headings. It is possible to group some of the latter into two products with 1968 sales above £10 million (for example, other wheat products and total maize products), but these were probably regarded as too heterogeneous for the measurement of concentration. Other products, such as semolina, barley products, rice products and soya meal, all had sales below £10 million in 1968. The exclusion of heterogeneous and small products probably accounts for most of the less than full coverage of the concentration data available. The exclusion of heterogeneous products is, of course, desirable and it is likely that the exclusion of small products has little effect on the average level of concentration reported, although it may slightly increase the average rise in concentration reported. These suppositions are of course based on the results found for the samples of products for which concentration data are available. It is possible that products with less than £10 million sales differ radically from larger products as far as concentration is concerned.

The number of products suppressed for disclosure reasons in both Censuses was very small. There were eight in the 1963 Census (gin, cigars, manufactured fuels, tinplate, data processing equipment, precious metals refining, flat glass, and plaster products) and six in the 1968 Census (five in inorganic chemicals: ammonia (in terms of 100 per cent NH_3) synthetic and by-products, chlorine, oxygen, phosphorous and phosphorous compounds, and silver compounds; in addition iron ore and ironstone were excluded from mining and quarrying). The eight products in 1963 accounted for less than 2 per cent of total sales by larger firms in that year, while the six products in 1968 accounted for even less sales, although it is not possible to calculate an exact percentage in this case. These exclusions can have had only an insignificant effect on the overall results. In so far as their exclusion does have an effect, it would tend to lower the average level of concentration because the products involved are highly concentrated.

Finally, some products were excluded at the initial selection of products. It is clear in a number of cases why this was so. Thus products with a high level of government participation, such as coal mining, were excluded. Similar considerations may have led also to the exclusion of aero-engines and locomotives in 1968; these products were however included in table 5 of the 1963 Census. Less understandable is the poor coverage of the shipbuilding industry: only one product from this industry was included in either year, accounting for 16.5 per cent of sales in 1963 and 14 per cent in 1968, while products such as war vessels, large tankers and cargo ships were omitted. The exclusion of the production of newspapers and magazines in both years is very difficult to understand.

Selection of 288 comparable products 1963–8

Products were omitted from the 340 noted on three grounds. First, twelve products were omitted because concentration ratios related to more than five firms. It is clear from the concentration ratios actually given that these products were highly concentrated and that five-firm ratios were not given for disclosure reasons. This being so, their exclusion from our comparison tends to give a small downward bias to the levels of concentration estimated from table 3.2. Secondly, 27 products have concentration ratios for 1968 only, the lack of data being due to census reclassification between 1963 and 1968. Thirdly, the period 1963–8 saw the Labour government's renationalisation of steel in March 1967. Since the primary task is to measure monopolistic trends in the private sector, it was necessary to omit all twelve products in the three industries affected: iron and steel (general), steel tubes, and iron castings, etc. In addition, coke, in the coal and petroleum products Order, was eliminated because of the effects of nationalisation.

Selection of 144 comparable products 1958–68

These products were selected as comparable by using the figures of 1963 total sales for each product given in the two Censuses; the ratio of 1963 sales in the 1963 Census to those in the 1968 Census was calculated for each product. Products were divided into five classes: (a) 109 products with a ratio of unity which were perfectly comparable; (b) 15 products with minor differences of less than 1 per cent, three of which had differences in five-firm sales rather than in total sales; (c) 20 products with differences of 1–5 per cent; (d) 36 products with differences greater than 5 per cent; (e) the remaining products which were non-comparable because of definitional changes. It was decided to use (a), (b) and (c) products in the sample. These 144 products represented 33 per cent of principal product sales in manufacturing and mining in 1968.

Selection of 256 comparable products 1968–75

The recent *Business Monitor PQ 1006* provides product concentration data for 340 products for 1963, 1968 and 1975, identified in Summary Table 44 of the 1968 Census. This additional information sheds no new light on the period 1963–8, but the figures for 1975 (which were calculated from the quarterly inquiries into manufacturers' sales) provide important new information on the concentration trend for the seven years 1968–75.

For our analysis, a sample of 256 comparable products was taken after applying the following exclusion procedures:

(a) Products in M L H industries iron and steel (general), steel tubes, iron castings and coke ovens were omitted because of the large public sector (the British Steel Corporation) in these industries. Fourteen products were omitted for this reason.

(b) Sixteen products were omitted because their concentration ratios were given for more than five firms in 1968 and/or in 1975. Their exclusion lowers the reported concentration means, since in eleven cases a 100 per cent concentration ratio was given for the total number of firms producing the product in 1975.

(c) The remaining 54 products were excluded either because of a change in product definition in 1975 (six cases), or because the 1975 concentration ratio was not given (25 cases), or because total sales in 1975 were not given (23 cases). This last exclusion procedure was used because a 1975 sales-weighted mean concentration ratio could not be calculated for these products. Also it was felt that non-publication of these 1975 sales figures may have arisen because of difficulties in comparing the sales of these product groups between 1968 and 1975. The effects of their omission are slight; the equally weighted C_5 being 64.5 per cent in 1968 and 66.2 per cent in 1975 for these 23 products, compared with values of 63.4 per cent and 65.1 per cent respectively for the 256-product sample. Their inclusion would have raised the level of concentration slightly, but left the small concentration rise observed for the equally weighted mean unchanged.

THE CLASSIFICATION OF PRODUCT
CONCENTRATION BY INDUSTRIAL ORDER

The samples of products discussed in chapter 3 were not random and it is possible that some types of industry are more heavily represented than are others, in which case the general results indicated by the average concentration ratios might not reflect changes in concentration in all industries in manufacturing and mining. To check this possibility, and to measure the effect of industrial type on the level and change in product concentration, this appendix classifies the comparable samples into eighteen Orders II–XIX in the 1968 SIC.

Table 3B.1 shows the mean level and change of concentration in each of the Orders for 1958–63 and 1963–8. Only means weighted by base-year sales have been recorded, since equally weighted means show similar results, only varying in minor detail. It should be stressed that each mean shows the average level of five-firm *product* concentration in each Order; it does *not* show the share of the five largest firms in the total sales of the Order.

1958–63

Within the 214-product sample in table 3B.1 only Order VII (mechanical engineering) appears to have had a fall in average product concentration in the period 1958–63. However, too much emphasis must not be placed on this result because the equally weighted mean concentration in the Order increased slightly by 0.1 percentage points. The appropriate conclusion to draw is that there was a small increase in mean product concentration for most Orders. Out of the sixteen Orders for which adequate information is available, a change of 4 percentage points or less was recorded in no less than eleven Orders. Order IV is omitted from the discussion because the data relate to only one product.

Five Orders experienced rises in product concentration of more than 4 percentage points: VIII (instrument engineering), II (mining and quarrying), XIII (textiles), XV (clothing and footwear) and III (food, drink and tobacco). The result for instrument engineering must be viewed with caution however, because only four products are classified in this group. But Order III, (food, drink and tobacco) stands out over this period: average product concentration rose by 11.1 percentage points in

135

just five years. The fact that this Order was by far the largest in terms of sales explains most of the large rise in the overall sales-weighted mean in the period.

Table 3B.1. *Changes in mean product concentration^a by 1968 SIC Order, 1958–63 and 1963–8*

		No. of products		Change in mean	
Order		1958–63	1963–8	1958–63	1963–8
				(percentages)	
II	Mining and quarrying	5	4	4.8	10.5
III	Food, drink and tobacco	28	41	11.1	2.8
IV	Coal and petroleum products	1	7	3.4	−2.9
V	Chemicals	14	39	1.2	2.5
VI	Metal manufacture	15	7	1.7	2.3
VII	Mechanical engineering	24	33	−1.1	4.5
VIII	Instrument engineering	4	5	5.8	1.5
IX	Electrical engineering	20	27	2.7	8.9
X	Shipbuilding	—	1	..	22.8
XI	Vehicles	9	8	4.0	5.9
XII	Metal goods n.e.s.	14	20	4.0	1.2
XIII	Textiles	26	28	5.3	9.3
XIV	Leather and fur	4	5	3.1	1.5
XV	Clothing and footwear	12	14	4.4	6.0
XVI	Bricks, pottery, etc.	13	16	2.7	7.2
XVII	Timber, furniture, etc.	5	9	0.9	0.2
XVIII	Paper, printing, etc.	10	10	1.7	1.2
XIX	Other manufacturing	10	14	0.3	2.1
	Total	214	288	4.0	4.1

SOURCES: See appendix 3A.
^{a} Means are weighted by base-year sales.

1963–8

The 288-product sample in table 3B.1 reveals only one Order with a fall in product concentration in the period 1963–8, namely, the high-concentration group of coal and petroleum products. In this case, the equally weighted mean confirms a fall in this group, as it confirms a rise in all the others. Nine of the seventeen available Orders had a small rise in product concentration. (Order X is omitted because the data relate to only one product). The nine ranged from Order XVII (timber, furniture, etc.) with a 0.2 percentage point rise, to Order III (food, drink and tobacco) with a below-average product concentration rise of 2.8 percentage points.

In this period, there is a more pronounced gap between the Orders with substantial increases in mean product concentration and the rest. Ignoring Order X, which had only one product concentration ratio, it can be seen that seven Orders had substantial increases in mean concentration: Orders II (10.5 points), VII (4.5 points), IX (8.9 points), XI (5.9 points), XIII

(9.3 points), XV (6.0 points), XVI (7.2 points). Order XV (clothing and footwear) is notable because it also experienced a substantial mean rise of 4.4 percentage points in 1958–63. On the other hand, the apparent small fall in product concentration in mechanical engineering in 1958–63 was followed by a substantial rise in 1963–8. Order II (mining and quarrying) had its substantial mean rise of 4.8 percentage points in 1958–63 overshadowed by the 10.5 percentage point rise of 1963–8. Textiles had a similar experience with a 5.3 percentage point rise followed by one of 9.3 percentage points. Both these groups, along with clothing and footwear, deserve special attention for their persistent rise in product concentration over both periods. Finally, electrical engineering had a mean rise of 8.9 percentage points in 1963–8, possibly reflecting the activities of the now defunct IRC.

1958–68

In order to identify the sectors of manufacturing which had large increases in product concentration in the whole ten years 1958–68 it is necessary to use the 144-product sample classified in table 3B.2. Six Orders stand out as

Table 3B.2. *Changes in mean product concentration^a by 1968 SIC Order, 1958–68*

Order		No. of products	Change in mean		
			1958–63	1963–8	1958–68
			(percentages)		
II	Mining and quarrying	4	4.0	10.5	14.5
III	Food, drink and tobacco	27	11.0	0.9	11.9
IV	Coal and petroleum products	—	—	—	—
V	Chemicals	7	−1.0	2.3	1.3
VI	Metal manufacture	4	−0.4	4.3	3.9
VII	Mechanical engineering	12	−4.1	6.6	2.5
VIII	Instrument engineering	1	2.8	−3.2	−0.4
IX	Electrical engineering	9	2.6	5.6	8.2
X	Shipbuilding	—	—	—	—
XI	Vehicles	6	3.8	5.9	9.7
XII	Metal goods n.e.s.	12	3.9	0.7	4.6
XIII	Textiles	20	5.4	10.9	16.3
XIV	Leather and fur	3	0.8	2.5	3.3
XV	Clothing and footwear	10	3.7	5.6	9.3
XVI	Bricks, pottery, etc.	9	2.0	4.1	6.1
XVII	Timber, furniture, etc.	4	0.5	2.2	2.7
XVIII	Paper, printing, etc.	10	1.6	1.2	2.8
XIX	Other manufacturing	6	0.7	1.6	2.3
	Total	144	4.4	5.1	9.5

SOURCES: See appendix 3A.
^{a} Means are weighted by mid-year sales.

having substantial or large increases in product concentration over the period. Orders XIII (textiles) and II (mining and quarrying) head the list with increases of 16.3 and 14.5 percentage points respectively. These Orders had medium to low product concentration in 1958 and experienced concentration rises in both periods, but much more in 1963–8. The experience of the Order ranked third on the list was quite different. Product concentration in Order III (food, drink and tobacco) was already above average in 1958; and most of the concentration increase in this decade occurred in 1958–63. The large increases in product concentration in Order XI (vehicles) and in Order XV (clothing, etc.) appear to be more evenly distributed over the two quinquennia although slightly faster in the second. In Order IX (electrical engineering) the rise in the period 1963–8 was even more marked. Thus the available product concentration information suggests that the main increases in market concentration in United Kingdom manufacturing occurred in these six Industrial Orders. However, the differences between *changes* in concentration in all Orders was not statistically significant, so there is no justification for stratifying the samples by industry group when measuring *changes* in product concentration.[1]

The differences in mean concentration levels between Orders are summarised in table 3B.3, which ranks each Order, except shipbuilding, by mean product concentration in 1968, as given by the 288-product sample in table 3B.1. Ranks in 1958 as given by the 214-product sample are also shown and it is assumed that coal and petroleum products ranked first in that year on the basis of the 1963 ranking. The rankings in both years are similar but there are four Orders which had a real change. Order XVIII (paper, printing and publishing), which experienced small increases in product concentration in the period, dropped from ninth to thirteenth, although this was largely due to the fact that a cluster of Orders had much the same product concentration levels. Order VI (metal manufacture) slipped from fifth to eighth, despite small increases in product concentration. On the other hand, Order VIII (instrument engineering) climbed from twelfth to ninth with larger increases. And finally, Order III (food, drink and tobacco) jumped from eighth to third position, largely as a result of an exceptionally large increase in product concentration in the period 1958–63.

Table 3B.3 reveals five Orders in which average product concentration exceeds the average of 67.5 per cent for manufacturing and mining as a

---

[1] If we compare 143 product concentration ratios (that is, excluding the one product in Order VIII) in 1958 and 1968, we cannot reject the null hypothesis (at the 5 per cent level) that there was no difference in average concentration *change* between Orders. The value of F for 14 and 128 degrees of freedom at the 5 per cent level is 1.76, compared with the calculated value of $F = 1.42$. This contrasts with the calculated $F = 8.77$ for the differences between Orders of the *level* of concentration in 1968.

Table 3B.3. *SIC (1968) Orders ranked by average level of product concentration in 1968*

	Rank		1968 mean concentration[a]
	1968	1958	
			(%)
Vehicles	(1)	(2)	95.5
Coal and petroleum products	(2)	(1)	92.1
Food, drink and tobacco	(3)	(8)	81.4
Electrical engineering	(4)	(4)	75.3
Chemicals	(5)	(7)	71.7
Bricks, pottery, etc.	(6)	(6)	66.9
Other manufacturing	(7)	(3)	64.7
Metal manufacture	(8)	(5)	64.5
Instrument engineering	(9)	(12)	59.5
Mining	(10)	(11)	54.2
Mechanical engineering	(11)	(10)	52.9
Metal goods n.e.s.	(12)	(13)	52.7
Paper, printing, etc.	(13)	(9)	52.5
Textiles	(14)	(15)	50.9
Clothing and footwear	(15)	(16)	33.2
Leather and fur	(16)	(14)	30.2
Timber, furniture, etc.	(17)	(17)	22.4
Total			67.5

SOURCES: See appendix 3A.
[a] Means are weighted by 1963 sales.

whole. Order XI (vehicles) and Order IV (coal and petroleum products) stand out at the top of the list with average product concentration ratios in excess of 90 per cent in 1968. Both groups undoubtedly headed the list in 1958 also, although data on coal and petroleum products are inadequate in that year. In 1963 it led the ranking according to the 288-product sample, and it is assumed in table 3B.3 that it also led in 1958. Third position in 1968 was held by Order III (food, drink and tobacco) with an average product concentration level of 81 per cent. As noted above, this group is a relative newcomer to the very high product concentration bracket, having in 1958 only just above-average product concentration. As already noted this elevation was accomplished largely in the period 1958–63. The other two high product concentration groups in 1968 were Order IX (electrical engineering), with a mean level of 75 per cent, and Order V (chemicals), with a mean level of 72 per cent. Both also had above-average product concentration levels in 1958. Product concentration appears to be highest in these five Orders and this is where the greatest challenge to competition is likely to exist.

Nine of the Orders in 1968 occupied the middle range between Order XVI (bricks, pottery etc.), with a mean ratio of 67 per cent, and Order

XIII (textiles), with a mean ratio of 51 per cent. This leaves only three Orders where atomistic competition may exist, namely XI (clothing and footwear), XIV (leather, leather goods and fur) and XVII (timber, furniture, etc.). In these three, the five largest firms produced on average less than one third of each product.

1968–75

The 256 comparable products for the period 1968–75 are classified according to Industrial Order in table 3B.4, and 1968 sales-weighted mean concentration ratios are given for 1968 and 1975. The overall increase in mean concentration of 1 percentage point in fact conceals some quite large changes in concentration by Order.

Table 3B.4. *Changes in mean product concentration by 1968 SIC Order, 1968–75*

Order		No. of products	Mean concentration[a]		
			1968	1975	Change 1968–75
			(percentages)		
II	Mining and quarrying	5	61.7	73.1	11.4
III	Food, drink and tobacco	37	70.3	72.1	1.8
IV	Coal and petroleum products	6	92.2	79.4	−12.8
V	Chemicals	30	69.0	70.1	1.1
VI	Metal manufacture	6	65.0	69.0	4.0
VII	Mechanical engineering	31	52.6	54.8	2.2
VIII	Instrument engineering	8	47.0	43.2	−3.8
IX	Electrical engineering	24	76.2	75.7	−0.5
X	Shipbuilding	1	57.4	45.7	−11.7
XI	Vehicles	7	94.2	91.9	−2.3
XII	Metal goods n.e.s.	17	47.7	50.6	2.9
XIII	Textiles	26	53.3	58.3	5.0
XIV	Leather and fur	5	28.1	39.7	11.6
XV	Clothing and footwear	13	32.9	33.3	0.4
XVI	Bricks, pottery, etc.	15	65.3	69.4	4.1
XVII	Timber, furniture, etc.	7	20.6	27.7	7.1
XVIII	Paper, printing, etc.	6	48.0	44.5	−3.5
XIX	Other manufacturing	12	63.4	63.2	−0.2
	Total	256	64.4	65.4	1.0

SOURCES: See appendix 3A.
[a] Weighted by 1968 sales.

Of the eleven Orders with average concentration increases, two stand out with more than an 11 percentage point increase in average concentration. These are mining and quarrying (Order II) which continued its large concentration increases of the 1960s into the 1970s apparently unabated, and leather and fur (Order XIV), a traditionally low-concentrated sector which previously showed little tendency to become more concentrated. Both sectors are small and, in the case of leather and fur where competitive conditions are typically prevalent, these large concentration increases may not be of important public concern. Such considerations also presumably apply to timber and furniture (Order XVII), which experienced the next largest increase in average concentration in the period of 7.1 percentage points. Notable concentration increases also occurred in textiles (Order XIII), bricks, pottery and glass (Order XVI) and metal manufacture (Order VI) continuing trends observed in the 1960s.

In contrast with the experience of the 1960s, however, the period 1968–75 was also characterised by a number of sectors with decreasing concentration. In particular, coal and petroleum products (Order IV) experienced a large fall in concentration of 12.8 percentage points between 1968 and 1975, a trend which was to some extent in evidence in the period 1963–8. The 11.7 percentage point decrease in concentration in shipbuilding (Order X) is of less interest, since only one product (maritime machinery) was included in this group. Instrument engineering (Order VIII) experienced a 3.8 percentage point concentration decrease in 1968–75 following increases from 1958 to 1968. Paper, printing and publishing (Order XVIII) and vehicles (Order XI) also had notable decreases after 1968 in contrast to their experience of increasing concentration up to 1968.

The post-1968 concentration experience therefore appears to have been much more varied than that of the period 1958–68. Not only did some sectors have falls as well as rises in the later period compared with the general tendency to increasing concentration over all manufacturing in 1958–68, but also some large concentration increases and decreases were observed in the period 1968–75. In this situation the change in average concentration over all manufacturing of 1 percentage point masks to some extent the dynamic changes in market structure occurring in different sectors.

PRODUCT AND INDUSTRY CONCENTRATION ACROSS ORDERS

It has already been shown in chart 1.1 that between 1958 and 1968 product (four-digit) and industrial (three-digit) concentration ratios had similar average increases, so that in this sense the two types of concentration ratio reveal the same trend and are substitutable. The classification of the two types of concentration ratio across Orders in appendices 2D and 3B enables us to correlate the change in the average product concentration ratio in each Order with the corresponding change in the average industrial concentration ratio to ascertain whether the two concentration ratios are good substitutes for each other.

Table 3C.1. *Regressions of industrial concentration changes on product concentration changes, 1958–63 and 1963–8[a]*

	Constant	b	r^2	n
Absolute change				
1958–63	0.37 (0.87)	1.10 (0.20)	0.68	16
1958–63[b]	1.58 (0.82)	0.58 (0.24)	0.31	15
1963–8	1.50 (1.30)	0.48 (0.26)	0.22	16
Percentage change				
1958–63	4.33 (3.01)	1.23 (0.30)	0.54	16
1958–63[b]	5.47 (2.77)	0.93 (0.30)	0.42	15
1963–8	5.19 (4.22)	0.65 (0.37)	0.18	16

[a] Standard errors in brackets.
[b] Omitting Order III.

Table 3C.1 reports the results of regressing the change in the employment-weighted mean industrial concentration ratio on the change in the sales-weighted mean product concentration ratio across Industrial Orders. The data for industry concentration ratios were taken from the final columns of table 2D.2 for 1958–63 and table 2D.3 for 1963–8. Orders IV (coal and petroleum products) and X (shipbuilding and marine engineering) were omitted because of their very small number of observations. Data for product concentration ratios for the same sixteen orders were taken from table 3B.1 for both 1958–63 and 1963–8.

It can be seen from table 3C.1 that the values of r^2 tend to be low, indicating that the two types of concentration ratio are not always good substitutes for each other. The highest values of r^2 observed for the sixteen sets of observations in 1958–63 are influenced by one extreme increase – Order III (food, drink and tobacco). When this observation is eliminated, r^2 becomes very low. However, it remains true that the regression coefficients are significantly greater than zero, using one-tailed t-tests at the 5 per cent level, and thus there is some association between the two types of concentration ratio. But because this association is not very strong, an increase in average industrial concentration in an Order is not always a good indicator of the corresponding increase in product concentration and the two types of concentration ratio should be analysed separately, as in the present book.

PLANT SIZE AND MINIMUM EFFICIENT SCALE

Estimates of the minimum efficient scale of plant based on hypothetical engineering data have been published for 49 industries in the United Kingdom.[1] For example, for oil refining in the first row of table 4A.1, the

Table 4A.1. *Plant size and minimum efficient scale, 1968*

	Employment, 1968		PS^b	Minimum efficient scale^c
	Median plant^a	Total		
	(thousands)		(percentages)	
Oil refining	1.30	17.2	7.6	7.3
Synthetic fibres	4.00	40.3	9.9	18.0
Beer^d	0.88	80.4	1.1	2.7
Bread	0.45	153.6	0.29	0.75
Cement^e	0.34	13.9	2.4	9.0
Bricks	0.15	58.3	0.25	0.6
Machine tools^f	0.40	72.1	0.56	0.75
Cotton spinning^g	0.36	85.6	0.42	2.0
Cotton weaving^g	0.20	63.7	0.31	2.0
Footwear	0.26	95.3	0.27	0.3
Sugar	1.25	15.0	8.3	14.0
Tobacco	4.25	40.8	10.4	21.0

^{a} Florence-median.
^{b} Florence-median as a percentage of total employment.
^{c} Output of plant as a percentage of total output.
^{d} Mean, excluding 13 per cent estimate.
^{e} Mean, excluding 1 per cent estimate.
^{f} Pratten, *Economies of Scale in Manufacturing*, p. 278.
^{g} *Ibid.* p. 238.

minimum efficient scale of plant is 7.3 per cent of total output. This figure was derived from technical information relating to the latest type of oil-refining plant, so that if we were building a new oil-refining industry from scratch there would be no need to have more than fourteen plants, provided that costs of transport were ignored. This proviso is important, because the costs of transporting inputs, or outputs, will often mean it is cheaper to use plants smaller than the technical minimum efficient scale but closer to the main centres of population.

[1] *A Review of Monopolies and Mergers Policy*, Cmnd 7198.

Because these figures are based on engineering data, rather than on the Census of Production, the definitions of some industries differ from those used in this book. In fact, it is possible to compare estimates of minimum efficient scale with the Florence-median plant size (PS) in only eleven cases. Table 4A.1 takes the means of the estimates in the Green Paper,[1] where more than one is given, or estimates by Pratten[2] in three cases. The estimated Florence-medians for 1968, which are medians of the first-moment distributions by employment, are expressed as percentages of the total employment in the industry. Except for oil refining the percentages are lower than those for the minimum efficient scale. This may be expected for several reasons.

First, PS is expressed as a percentage of employment whereas the minimum efficient scale is a percentage of output. As costs decrease to reach the minimum efficient scale of output, we should expect a 1 per cent increase in output to be achieved with a less than 1 per cent increase in employment, until the output at which average labour productivity is maximised. After this point average total costs may continue to fall because of falling average fixed costs and/or because average productivity of other inputs continues to rise. But until this point is reached, the ratio of output to labour tends to increase with the size of plant and the optimum size would tend to be higher measured in terms of output than in terms of employment. Furthermore, two plants, A and B, may have much the same levels of employment, but plant A may be more efficient than plant B because it has more output, having reached the production frontier, whereas plant B is still moving towards this extreme. The size distribution of plants by output would be more relevant to the measurement of economies of scale but the distribution of plants by employment is all that is published in the Census of Production. It is worth noting that the census figures of net output *per capita*, classified by size of establishment measured by employment, cannot be used to measure economies of scale of plant because of the well-known Steindl paradox, namely that completely different estimates of the relationship between labour productivity and size of plant may be obtained by using the numerator (output) or the denominator (labour) as a measure of size.[3] For the same reason we cannot use the cost disadvantage ratio[4] in any measure of economies of scale.

Secondly, the published size distributions are affected by transport costs, whereas the minimum efficient scale percentages exclude these effects and

[1] *Ibid.* pp. 87–8.

[2] C. F. Pratten, *Economies of Scale in Manufacturing Industry*, Cambridge University Press, 1971.

[3] See J. Steindl, *Maturity and Stagnation in American Capitalism*, Oxford, Blackwell, 1952, and J. Johnston, 'Labour productivity and size of establishment', *Bulletin of the Oxford University of Statistics*, vol. 16, 1954.

[4] Proposed by R. E. Caves, J. Khalilzadeh-Shirazi and M. E. Porter, 'Scale economies in statistical analyses of market-power', *Review of Economics and Statistics*, vol. 57, 1975.

thereby overestimate that minimum scale of plant which is efficient in terms of both production and transport costs. Thirdly, the observed distributions are affected by old vintage equipment and by techniques which may have been of 'best practice' in the past but which are now inferior. Assuming that technical progress tends to increase the optimum size of plant, it follows that the estimates of the minimum efficient scale, based on the hypothetical costs of future techniques and of the most recent vintage of capital equipment, will tend to exceed the estimates of plant size derived from the *ex post* size distributions.

The pairs of estimates are broadly consistent. Both columns suggest that plant economies of scale are important in oil refining and in synthetic fibres, but are unimportant in bread, bricks, machine tools, cotton spinning and weaving, and footwear. They appear to be inconsistent in the case of cement, but one of the reasons for this is that the estimates of the minimum efficient scale exclude the effects of transport costs. A second reason is that fluctuations in regional demand for cement tend to limit the size of plant built in any one location: cement plants are expensive and there is no point in having one which the engineers suggest has the minimum efficient scale if its output is needed only occasionally owing to fluctuations in demand. Finally, there is an apparent inconsistency in the case of beer, where the estimates suggest that there should be only 37 breweries in the country. Once again part of the difference may be explained by transport costs. Part is also attributable to the use of old equipment and techniques in some existing breweries. But consumers' tastes differ, and if many people prefer the quality of the product of old plants using traditional techniques to the beer produced by modern plants using all the latest techniques of chemical engineering, it is possible that the minimum efficient scale from a technical point of view is too large from an economic point of view. So the differences between minimum efficient scale and PS in the cement and beer industries cannot be used to support an argument that the Florence-median underestimates the optimum scale of plant.

The rank correlation coefficient between the plant size percentages and those of the minimum efficient scale in table 4A.1 is 0.967, which is significantly different from zero. With eleven observations we would require Σd_i^2 to exceed 83.6, where d_i is the ith difference in rank order, in order to accept the null hypothesis (at the 5 per cent level of significance) that the population rank correlation is zero.[1] In fact, $\Sigma d_i^2 = 6$, which is far below the critical level.

Further support for the median of the first-moment size distribution of

[1] $\Sigma d_i^2 = 83.6$ is equivalent to a sample rank correlation of 0.62, as shown by E. G. Olds, 'The 5% significance levels for sums of squares of rank differences and a correction', *Annals of Mathematical Statistics*, vol. 20, 1949.

plants as a measure of plant economies of scale comes from a comparison with the separate estimates of optimum size made by Rees[1] using the survivor technique. His sample of 30 industries for 1968 and the sample of 76 used in chapter 4 overlap in 21 cases. The linear regression of PS on the Rees optimum size is 0.76 (0.15) with $r^2 = 0.57$. The logarithmic regression is 0.87 (0.14) with $r^2 = 0.67$. The agreement is good enough for our purposes. The average value of the Florence-median for these industries was 590 employees, compared with 683 employees using the estimates by Rees. There is no reason to suppose that survivor technique estimates are more reliable than the Florence-median. Indeed, as mentioned in chapter 4, survivor technique estimates are usually calculated from univariate size distributions of plants, whereas bivariate size distributions, summarising the sizes of the same plants at two dates, are required before any reasonable assessment can be made of the tendency for a particular size of plant to survive. If we have to choose between the two measures, there is a good case for preferring the Florence-median, at least to indicate the variation of optimum plant size between industries, on the grounds that estimates can be made for all industries from the univariate size distributions which are normally published.

The general conclusion is that the very limited data available justify the use of PS as a measure of plant economies of scale in a regression analysis to determine the level of industrial concentration; differences between the values of PS across industries reflect differences in plant economies of scale between industries. The median of the first-moment distribution of plants by employment is a good measure of the central tendency of the size distribution of plants, for it is not affected by extreme size of plants nor by the numbers of plants. The central tendency of the distribution can be regarded as reflecting plant economies of scale; large values indicate a large optimum size of plant, whereas small values suggest that plant economies of scale are unimportant.

---

[1] Rees, 'Optimum plant size'.

SOME ECONOMETRIC PROBLEMS

Numerators and denominators

The dependent variable, $\log C_5$, in table 4.1 is the logarithm of the ratio of the employment of the five largest enterprises to the total employment of each industry. If z_i is the employment of the ith enterprise in an industry, $(i = 1, \ldots, n)$, ranked in descending order of size, then

$$\log C_5 = \log \sum_{i=1}^{5} z_i - \log \sum_{i=1}^{n} z_i \tag{4B.1}$$

where $\sum_{i=1}^{n} z_i = E$, industry size

The logarithm of the denominator is one of the explanatory variables in table 4.1. It might be objected, therefore, that the negative and significant partial correlation between $\log C_5$ and $\log E$ in table 4.1 is merely statistical, stemming from the fact that E appears as the denominator of C_5. We do not think this objection is important, if only because the simple correlation between $\log C_5$ and $\log E$ is very low, with $r^2 = 0.052$. The other explanatory variables in table 4.1 are not affected by $\log E$.

Near-identities and identification

For twenty years research workers have been concerned about the possibility that a regression equation purporting to explain variations in concentration merely reflects an identity or near-identity. Here we consider the estimates in the second column of table 4.1 when the size distributions of enterprises and of plants are approximately log-normal *within* each industry. The proportion of the total number of enterprises in an industry represented by the five largest is given approximately by $(n-5)/n = \Lambda(z_6|\mu,\sigma^2)$, where μ and σ^2 are the mean and variance of $\log_e z$, and the value of C_5 is derived from the first-moment distribution function by $C_5 = 1 - \Lambda_1(z_6|\mu+\sigma^2,\sigma^2)$. If we know n and σ^2 we can calculate C_5, from equation (4B.2).

$$v_{0q} - \sigma = v_{1q} \tag{4B.2}$$

where v_{0q} is the normal equivalent deviate of $(n-5)/n$, and v_{1q} is the normal deviate of $1-C_5$. For example, suppose $n=100$, so that $(n-5)/n=\Lambda(z_6|\mu,\sigma^2)=0.95$, then $v_{0q}=1.645$, since 95 per cent of the area of the standard normal curve $\Phi(0,1)$ lies to the left of the point 1.645 deviations above the zero mean. If $\sigma=2.17$, then $v_{1q}=-0.525$, so that $1-C_5=0.30$, since 30 per cent of the area of $\Phi(0,1)$ lies to the left of the point -0.525 deviations below the zero mean. Hence $C_5=70$ per cent and is clearly determined by n and σ^2.

The logarithm of total employment is given by $\log_e E = \log_e n + \mu + \frac{1}{2}\sigma^2$ and, assuming the size distribution of establishments is also log-normal, the logarithm of the Florence-median plant size (PS) is given by $\log_e PS = \mu_p + \sigma_p^2$. The logarithm of the arithmetic mean size of plant is $\mu_p + \frac{1}{2}\sigma_p^2$, so that $\log_e E = \log_e m + \mu_p + \frac{1}{2}\sigma_p^2$, where m is the number of establishments. These results may be used to rewrite the regression equation in the second column of table 4.1.

$$\begin{aligned}\log_e C_5 &= \log_e \alpha + \beta \log_e PS - \gamma \log_e E + \delta \log_e(m/n) + \varepsilon \qquad (4\text{B}.3)\\ &= \log_e \alpha + \beta(\mu_p+\sigma_p^2) - \gamma(\log_e n + \mu + \frac{1}{2}\sigma^2) + \delta \log_e(m/n) + \varepsilon\\ &= \log_e \alpha - \gamma \log_e n + \frac{1}{2}(\delta-\gamma)\sigma^2 + (\beta-\frac{1}{2}\delta)\sigma_p^2 + (\delta-\gamma)\mu + (\beta-\delta)\mu_p + \varepsilon\end{aligned}$$

Thus $\log_e C_5$ depends negatively on $\log_e n$ and positively on σ^2 since $\hat\delta > \hat\gamma$ in table 4.1. An increase in n increases v_{0q} and hence increases v_{1q} given σ, and this in turn implies a decrease in C_5; again, given n, an increase in σ decreases v_{1q} and this implies an increase in C_5. Thus it could be argued that the regression resulting from the specification in (4B.3) merely reflects the variation in n and σ between industries in which the size distributions of enterprises tend to be log-normal.

However, even if the size distributions are log-normal, there are still terms in μ, μ_p and σ_p^2 in the third line of (4B.3) which are not mathematically related to C_5. Note that the variance of the logarithms of plant sizes, σ_p^2, differs from the variance of the logarithms of enterprise sizes, σ^2. Secondly, the mathematical relationship between n, σ and C_5 in (4B.2) depends on normal equivalent deviates and is not the same as the logarithmic and semi-logarithmic relationships between these variables in (4B.3). Thirdly, while the log-normal distribution tends to be a good approximation to observed size distributions as a whole, the fit is not perfect and in the extreme upper tails, which are relevant to C_5, the fit is not good enough to provide reliable estimates of C_5 using (4B.2). Instead of using (4B.2) the estimates of C_5 made in chapter 2 were derived from the upper tails of the observed size distributions using a graphic method rather than a log-normal approximation. Fourthly, the use of changes in the logarithms of these variables in table 4.2 yields values of $\bar R^2$ which are very low for a near-identity. Moreover, the addition of the mergers variable, which is excluded from (4B.3), significantly increases $\bar R^2$ and this would be most unlikely if the other variables explained nearly all the variation in $\log_e C5$ in a near-identity.

For all these reasons, we do not think that the basic regression results in chapter 4 can be attributed to a near-identity stemming from the log-normal relationship in (4B.2). The estimated relationship between concentration, Florence-median plant size, employment and the plant–enterprise ratio is not merely the statistical result of near-identities; on the contrary, it reflects the economic effects of the explanatory variables on the dependent variable.

Mean change and analysis of variance of concentration changes in table 4.2

The dependent variable in table 4.2 is $\log_e C5$ (1968) $-\log_e C5$ (1958) and the arithmetic mean value of the 76 observations is 0.2787, which corresponds to an increase in the geometric mean concentration ratio of about 32 per cent, since the antilog (to base e) of 0.2787 is 1.32. This exceeds the 24 per cent increase in the arithmetic mean, given by $\Sigma C5$ (1968)$/\Sigma C5$ (1958), which is $45.6/36.9 = 1.236$, using data on 79 comparable industries from table 2.5 in chapter 2. The arithmetic mean of the ratios of $C5$ (1968) to $C5$ (1958) for each industry, given by $(1/n)\Sigma[C5$ (1968)$/C5$(1958)], cannot be less than the geometric mean of 1.32, and must therefore increase by at least 8 percentage points more than the 24 per cent increase obtained from table 2.5. Thus the regressions in table 4.2, which relate to changes in concentration of individual industries, cannot be used to decompose the increase in average concentration from 36.9 per cent in 1958 to 45.6 per cent in 1968 recorded in table 2.5.

Nor can we measure the contributions of the initial concentration level and mergers to the mean change in the dependent variable in table 4.2; while the regression coefficients on the logarithms of these two variables are independent of units of measurement, the mean values of these variables are influenced by the units used and hence we cannot use $\bar{Y} = \hat{\alpha} + \Sigma \hat{\beta}_i' \bar{X}_i$ $(i = 1, \ldots, 5)$ to assess the importance of these two explanatory variables. Note that even if we were able to overcome the problems created by units of measurement, we should not be able to overcome the problem of assessing the importance of stochastic factors using this method, since the mean of the residuals is zero.

However, it is possible to provide an analysis of variance table to show the relative contributions of each of the explanatory variables to the variation of the dependent variable between industries, as given in table 4B.1. We must stress that this conventional approach has its limitations. For example, consider the two-variable case. If merger expenditure in each industry doubles, the variance of the logarithms of this variable $\hat{\sigma}_x^2$, stays the same. Denoting the logarithm of the change in concentration by y_i, with variance $\hat{\sigma}_y^2$, the equation $\hat{\sigma}_y^2 = \beta \hat{\sigma}_x^2 / \hat{\rho}^2$, where $\hat{\rho}$, is the correlation coefficient, is also unchanged. Thus the traditional analysis of the total variation in y would not reveal any effects from doubling of the mergers expenditure. With this warning in mind, let us consider the analysis of variance in table 4B.1.

Table 4B.1. *Analysis of variance of logarithmic concentration changes across 76 comparable industries, 1958–68*

	Degrees of freedom	Sum of squares	Mean square
Concentration 1958	1	1.720	1.720
Addition of: Economies of scale Industry size Plant–enterprise ratio	3	1.337	0.446
Regression	4	3.057	0.764
Addition of mergers	1	0.365	0.365
Regression	5	3.422	0.684
Residual	70	4.356	0.0622
Total	75	7.778	0.1037

The highest zero order correlation is -0.4702 between the dependent variable and the logarithm of concentration in 1958. As shown in the first row of table 4B.1, this variable contributed some 22 per cent of the total sum of squares of the dependent variable. The addition of the three variables used to explain the level of concentration in chapter 4 (economies of scale, industry size, plant–enterprise ratio) adds another 17 per cent to the sum of squares column. The zero order correlations between the dependent variable and each of these three explanatory variables are respectively 0.276, -0.282, 0.107, so the plant–enterprise ratio is the least important of the three. The zero order correlation between the dependent variable and mergers expenditure is 0.125 and its inclusion in the regressin adds 4.6 per cent to the sum of squares column. Although this is statistically significant, it is very small, having approximately the same effect as the average of the three explanatory variables just discussed.

It must be stressed that this does not imply that between 1958 and 1968 mergers were responsible for only 4.6 per cent of the average increase in concentration. The use of mergers expenditure at the Order (two-digit) level to measure merger activity at the industry (three-digit) level obviously underestimates the effects of mergers. Furthermore, the analysis of variance in table 4B.1 reflects variations between industries rather than the average experience of industries.

The mean value of the mergers variable was 2.8093, which after taking antilogarithms (to base e) corresponds to a geometric mean mergers expenditure of 16.6 per cent of initial assets. We may estimate the average merger effect as $(0.0811)(2.8093) = 0.2278$, compared with the actual mean concentration increase of 0.2787. Thus if average mergers expenditure had been 1 per cent instead of 16.6 per cent of initial assets, the dependent variable would have been 0.0509 $(0.2787-0.2278)$. This point estimate is surrounded by a 95 per cent confidence interval of ± 0.1647 so our estimate of the effects of mergers is not precise. Moreover, mergers expenditure was not the only important variable. The level of concentration had an important negative effect on the increase in concentration. If the geometric mean concentration ratio in 1958 had been 10 percentage points lower, the mean increase in concentration would have been 0.3787, or 46 per cent instead of 32 per cent. Thus we would argue that mergers expenditure played an important part in increasing concentration in 1958–68, but this part cannot be estimated as 81 per cent, using 0.2278/0.2787, because other variables, particularly $\log_e C_5$ (1958), were also important.

SOURCES OF DATA
FOR CHAPTER 4

The data used in chapter 4 were as follows:

C_5: estimates of five-enterprise employment concentration discussed in chapter 2 above.

PS: estimates of the median of the first-moment distribution of plants by employment, made in the bulk of cases arithmetically by linear interpolation. In a few cases extrapolation was necessary and this was done graphically on log–probability paper. The sources of the data were: for 1958, Summary Table 4 of 1958 Census of Production (part 133) and for 1968, table 2 of the individual industry reports in the 1968 Census.

PN: the ratio of all plants to all firms as given in Summary Table 1 of the 1968 Census of Production for 1968 figures, and the 1963 Census of Production for 1958 figures.

E: total employment in all firms taken from Summary Tables 1 of the 1968 and 1963 Censuses of Production.

M: the ratio of net assets transferred in 1958–68 to net assets at end-1957 (as a percentage). The data refer to quoted companies with assets in excess of £0.5 million at the beginning of 1961. Data are at the industry group level, the same value being given to each industry in a group.[1]

ADV: the ratio of advertising expenditure to sales in 1968 (as a percentage). Of the 76 industries in our comparable sample, individual observations were available in 34 cases. The remaining observations refer to the group (between the MLH and Order level of aggregation) of which the industries were a part. The data sources were Summary Tables 1 and 4 of the 1968 Census of Production.

As indicated in the text, change variables ΔC_5, ΔPS, ΔPN and ΔE were measured as the ratio of the 1968 to the 1958 values.

---

[1] They were taken from Department of Trade and Industry, *A Survey of Mergers: 1958–68*, appendices 1 and 2, London, HMSO, 1970.

SOURCES OF DATA
FOR CHAPTER 5

Five-enterprise concentration ratios for 1958, 1963 and 1968 are given in table 5A.1 for a random sample of 30 products. Unfortunately comparable data for 1968 are not available for all the sample. There are 23 products for

Table 5A.1. *Random sample of 30 products* Percentages

MLH (1968)		Sales concentration ratios (C_5)			
		1958	1963	1968	1975
212	Flour confectionery	26.7	51.0	60.1	64.2
239 (1)	Blended whisky	96.1	94.2	91.0	87.1
271 (2)	Organic chemicals	59.3	64.9	63.2	..
275	Detergents	90.4	84.5	79.9	82.8
311	Steel blooms, billets and slabs	72.2	69.6	96.6	..
336	Contractors' plant	38.2	38.2	39.7	..
339 (1)	Mining machinery	36.2	42.2	59.1	..
339 (5,6,8,9)	Pulp-making machinery, etc.	84.0	93.8	83.3	82.5
341 (1)	Boilers and boilerhouse plant	69.8	60.3	61.7	..
362	Insulated wires and cables	53.3	68.0	81.8	..
363	Telephone installations	90.4	94.0	96.4	98.9
363	Line apparatus	93.9	96.2	99.9	94.9
354	Electronic testing equipment	46.7	36.9	..	..
368	Washing machines	76.4	85.2	86.9	100.0[a]
381	Trailers and caravans	37.0	43.5	44.2	34.6
412	Flax	38.2	46.8	55.6	..
414 (1)	Wool sorting, etc.	39.2	42.5	50.0	72.3
415	Jute, yarn and cloth	47.7	55.6[b]	68.9	73.4
417	Hosiery, etc.	15.0	21.2	33.2	40.2
419	Woven carpets	41.2	42.3	57.5	..
419	Other carpets	65.6	55.0	54.4	..
421 (1)	Narrow fabrics (elastic)	59.0	59.1	74.3[c]	..
421 (2,3)	Narrow fabrics (non-elastic)	22.5	26.0	31.3	35.6
429 (1)	Asbestos manufactures	77.4	82.4	86.2	86.7
431 (2)	Fellmongery	46.1	42.7	42.2	50.6
444	Heavy overalls and aprons	24.7	26.7[b]	27.4	32.6
446	Hats, caps and millinery	24.0	29.5	36.1	34.3
449 (1,3,4)	Corsets and brassieres	30.8	38.0	59.0	63.2
471	Builders' woodwork	19.2	18.4	23.0	32.9
484 (1)	Wallpaper	91.6	95.1[b]	89.7	74.1

[a] C_7.
[b] Ratios in the 1968 Census differed from these figures as follows: jute, 59.2; heavy overalls 26.0; and wallpaper 95.6   [c] Not comparable with earlier data.

154

which five-enterprise ratios were published in Summary Table 44 of the 1968 Census. Of these, nineteen products were prima facie completely comparable; one (wallpaper) had a minor revision in 1963 sales of less than 1 per cent; one (heavy overalls and aprons, and jeans) had a less than 5 per cent 1963 sales revision; and one (jute) had a revision of just over 5 per cent. The figures for 1963 in table 5A.1 are the earlier ones, the revised estimates being shown in a footnote. Inspection of the individual industry reports revealed that one product (narrow fabrics (elastic)) was substantially redefined in 1968, and this product was omitted from the comparisons in chapter 5.

Concentration ratios for 1968 for six of the remaining seven products were kindly provided by the BSO. These products were: organic chemicals, contractors' plant, wires and cables, flax, woven carpets, and other carpets. These BSO data are not always strictly comparable with the earlier data, but the discrepancies were minor. One product (electronic testing equipment) was so radically redefined in 1968 that its concentration ratio could not be recovered and hence it was omitted. Finally, the product group steel blooms, billets and slabs was omitted in the comparisons of chapter 5 because of the effect of steel nationalisation in raising C_5 from 69.6 to 96.6 per cent in the period 1963–8.

Product concentration ratios for 1975 are available for nineteen of the random sample but they were published too late for us to prepare case studies for the period 1968 to 1975. These ratios are also shown in table 5A.1.

APPENDIX 6A

SOURCES AND METHODS,
CHAPTER 6

Prices and industrial concentration

Prices: Laspeyres indices of prices for most products in 1958, 1963 and 1968 were obtained from the index of wholesale prices published annually in *Trade and Industry*. They were supplemented by unpublished data kindly made available by the Department of Industry and the Ministry of Agriculture, Food and Fisheries.

Wages: the average employee compensation per operative was taken from the Summary Tables of the Census of Production. The level is heavily influenced by the proportion of females but there is no reason to suppose that this proportion influenced the percentage change in average wages.

Other costs per unit of output: these were taken from the Census of Production. They include raw-material costs and costs of packaging and fuel. The increase in these costs was corrected for changes in real output by dividing by the current value of net output deflated by the price index used above.

Labour productivity: the value of net output *per capita* in current prices is given in the Census and the proportionate change in this was deflated by the price index used above to give the proportionate increase in real output *per capita*.

Concentration: the measure used was the percentage of industry employment accounted for by the five largest enterprises by employment, as described in chapter 2. C_5 was calculated by extrapolation from the cumulative forms of the size distributions of enterprises by employment published by the Census of Production for each industry.

Profitability and concentration

Hart and Morgan[1] used multiple logarithmic regressions to explain variation in the rate of profit in value added across industries. For purposes of comparison, table 6A.1 gives the results of multiple linear regressions using the data in Hart and Morgan, which also describes the sources used. The simple regression coefficient on concentration is 0.00159 ($\pm$0.00039),

[1] Hart and Morgan, 'Market structure and economic performance'.

156

since table 6A.1 multiplies the raw coefficients by 100 to simplify presentation, and $R^2 = 0.126$.

Table 6A.1. *Linear regressions of profitability on concentration and other variables, 113 industries, United Kingdom 1968*

	Equation number[a]			
	(1)	(2)	(3)	(4)
Concentration ratio[b]	0.159[c]	0.067	0.052	0.056
	(0.039)	(0.042)	(0.038)	(0.037)
Capital–labour ratio, proxy[b]		0.024[c]	0.024[c]	0.024[c]
		(0.006)	(0.005)	(0.005)
Entry barrier[b]		0.001	0.001	
		(0.001)	(0.001)	
Import–sales ratio[b]		−0.016	0.013	
		(0.054)	(0.049)	
Demand change			0.026	0.027
‹			(0.020)	(0.020)
Advertising–sales ratio			2.143[c]	2.129[c]
			(0.402)	(0.400)
R^2	0.126	0.266	0.430	0.428

[a] Standard errors in brackets.
[b] Coefficient and standard error multiplied by 100.
[c] Coefficient significantly different from zero at 5 per cent level.

Wages and industrial concentration

The sample used to examine inter-industry wage differentials in table 6.5 was determined by the availability of data, and, in particular, by the need to reconcile data from the *Department of Employment Gazette*, the *New Earnings Survey* and the Census of Production.

The main problem with the data arose with respect to the number of working days lost per 1000 employees (TUA), which was taken from the February 1976 *Department of Employment Gazette*. Individual observations were not available for 46 of the 138 industries, thus reducing the sample size to 92. A further seventeen industries had to be eliminated in order to use the variable for skill (SK). Finally, the remaining 75 industries were reduced by 26 to 49 in order that individual observations on male manual workers not subject to collective agreement (NCA) might be used. These data were taken from the *New Earnings Survey* for 1973, table 110. Data on hourly earnings (HE) were taken from the *New Earnings Survey* for 1970 for the sample of 49 industries, although in just under half of these cases they are at a less disaggregated level than the MLH. The 49 industries represent a third of manufacturing industry, and although they were not selected randomly, there appears to be no obvious reason why they should not be representative.

Hourly earnings relate to full-time manual men aged 21 or over in April 1970, taken from the *New Earnings' Survey*, 1970, table 18. Figures are available for 26 industries, whilst in the remaining 23 cases they relate to groups of industries of which the relevant industry is a part.

Skill (SK) is the proportion of total male employees (rather than total male operatives) who were classified as skilled operatives on 18 May 1969, taken from the *Employment and Productivity Gazette*, January 1969, table 24.

TUA is the number of working days lost per 1000 employees on average in the three years 1966–8, taken from the *Department of Employment Gazette*, February 1976, table 7. The averaging process was used to iron out the effects of stoppages in any one year. The data relate to all employees. Alternative variables tried were: TUB, the number of working days lost per 1000 employees in 1968 only; TUC, the number of stoppages per 100,000 employees on average for 1966–8; and TUD the same for 1968 only. Each variable gave a similar result so that only results using TUA are reported.

NCA is the percentage of full-time manual men, aged 21 and over, not subject to collective agreement in April 1973, taken from the *New Earnings Survey*, 1973, table 110. 1973 was the first year for which such data were collected.

The variable for region is the percentage of employment in the more prosperous regions (East and West Midlands, East Anglia, and South East England) in all establishments in 1968, taken from Summary Table 27, part 157 of the 1968 Census. In a number of cases, the BSO withheld data for one or more of the relevant regions for disclosure reasons. In such cases the remainder of employment was allocated equally between regions for which data were withheld on the assumption that the one or two firms involved in each case were likely to be of approximately the same size.

Efficiency and concentration

The basic source was *Economic Trends*, March 1974, pp. xxxiii–xliv. Company-funded current expenditure on R & D was from column 2, table H; output from column 2 of table C; turnover from column 5 of table B. The formal regression of the first column of table 6.8 on the third column was $RD = 2.23+0.123C5$ $(r^2 = 0.50)$. This indicates the strength of the positive association which appeared in the scatter diagram, but it must not be used to relate R & D expenditure to $C5$ for reasons given in chapter 6.

INDEX

RECENT PUBLICATIONS OF THE
NATIONAL INSTITUTE OF ECONOMIC
AND SOCIAL RESEARCH

published by
THE CAMBRIDGE UNIVERSITY PRESS

ECONOMIC AND SOCIAL STUDIES
  XXVI   *Urban Development in Britain: Standards, Costs and Resources, 1964–2004*
      By P. A. STONE. Vol. I: *Population Trends and Housing.* 1970. pp. 436. £14.75 net.
  XXVII *The Framework of Regional Economics in the United Kingdom*
      By A.J.BROWN. 1972. pp. 372. £15.00 net.
  XXVIII *The Structure, Size and Costs of Urban Settlements*
      By P. A. STONE. 1973. pp. 304. £12.00 net.
  XXIX *The Diffusion of New Industrial Processes: An International Study*
      Edited by L. NABSETH and G. F. RAY. 1974. pp. 346. £13.50 net.
  XXX *The Evolution of Giant Firms in Britain*
      By S. J. PRAIS. 1976. pp. 340. £12.00 net.
  XXXI *British Economic Policy 1960–74*
      Edited by F. T. BLACKABY. 1978. pp. 710. £24.00 net.
  XXXII *Industrialisation and the Basis for Trade*
      By R. A. BATCHELOR, R. L. MAJOR and A. D. MORGAN. 1980. pp. 380. £17.50 net.

OCCASIONAL PAPERS
  XXV *The Analysis and Forecasting of the British Economy*
      By M. J. C. SURREY. 1971. pp. 120. £5.25 net.
  XXVI *Mergers and Concentration in British Industry*
      By P. E. HART, M. A. UTTON and G. WALSHE. 1973. pp. 190. £7.25 net.
  XXVII *Recent Trends in Monopoly in Great Britain*
      By G. WALSHE. 1974. pp. 156. £6.75 net.
  XXVIII *Cyclical Indicators for the Postwar British Economy*
      By D. J. O'DEA. 1975. pp.184. £8.10 net.
  XXIX *Poverty and Progress in Britain, 1953–73*
      By G. C. FIEGEHEN, P. S. LANSLEY and A. D. SMITH. 1977. pp. 192. £8.50 net.
  XXX *The Innovation Process in the Energy Industries*
      By G. F. RAY and L. UHLMANN. 1979. pp. 132. £6.00 net.
  XXXI *Diversification and Competition*
      By M. A. UTTON. 1979. pp. 124. £6.95 net.

NIESR STUDENTS' EDITION
  1 *Growth and Trade* (abridged from *Industrial Growth and World Trade*)
      By A. MAIZELS. 1970. pp. 312. £4.75 net.
  2 *The Antitrust Laws of the U.S.A* (2nd edition, unabridged)
      By A. D. NEALE. 1970. pp. 544. £7.25 net.
  4 *British Economic Policy 1960–74: Demand Management* (an abridged version of *British Economic Policy 1960–74*)
      Edited by F. T. BLACKABY. 1979. PP.4/2. £7.50 NET.

REGIONAL PAPERS
  1 *The Anatomy of Regional Activity Rates* by JOHN BOWERS, and *Regional Social Accounts for the United Kingdom* by V. H. WOODWARD. 1970. pp. 192. £5.50 net.

163

2 *Regional Unemployment Differences in Great Britain* by P. C. CHESHIRE, and *Interregional Migration Models and their Application to Great Britain* by R. WEEDEN. 1973. pp. 118. £5.50 net.

3 *Unemployment, Vacancies and the Rate of Change of Earnings: A Regional Analysis* by A. E. WEBB, and *Regional Rates of Employment Growth: An Analysis of Variance Treatment* by R. WEEDEN. 1974. pp. 114. £5.50 net.

THE NATIONAL INSTITUTE OF ECONOMIC AND
SOCIAL RESEARCH

publishes regularly

THE NATIONAL INSTITUTE ECONOMIC REVIEW

A quarterly analysis of the general economic situation in the United Kingdom and the world overseas, with forecasts eighteen months ahead. The last issue each year contains an assessment of medium-term prospects. There are also in most issues special articles on subjects of interest to academic and business economists.

Annual subscriptions, £25.00 (home), and £35.00 (abroad), also single issues for the current year, £7.00 (home) and £10.00 (abroad), are available directly from NIESR, 2 Dean Trench Street, Smith Square, London, SW1P 3EH.

Subscriptions at the special reduced price of £10.00 p.a. are available to students in the United Kingdom and Irish Republic on application to the Secretary of the Institute.

Back numbers and reprints of issues which have gone out of stock are distributed by Wm. Dawson and Sons Ltd., Cannon House, Park Farm Road, Folkestone. Microfiche copies for the years 1959–79 are available from EP Microform Ltd, Bradford Road, East Ardsley, Wakefield, Yorks.

Published by
HEINEMANN EDUCATIONAL BOOKS
AN INCOMES POLICY FOR BRITAIN
Edited by FRANK BLACKABY. 1972. pp. 260. £4.00 net.
THE UNITED KINGDOM ECONOMY
By the NIESR. 4th edn, 1979. pp. 128. £1.80 net.
DEMAND MANAGEMENT
Edited by MICHAEL POSNER. 1978. pp. 256. £9.50 (hardback), £4.50 (paperback) net.
DE-INDUSTRIALISATION
Edited by FRANK BLACKABY. 1979. pp. 282. £9.50 (hardback), £5.50 (paperback) net.
BRITAIN'S TRADE AND EXCHANGE-RATE POLICY
Edited by ROBIN MAJOR. 1979. pp. 240. £9.75 (hardback), £5.50 (paperback) net.

LIBRARY OF DAVIDSON COLLEGE

Books on regular loan may be checked out for two weeks. Books must be presented at the Circulation Desk in order to be renewed.

A fine is charged after date due.

Special books are subject to special regulations at the discretion of the library staff.